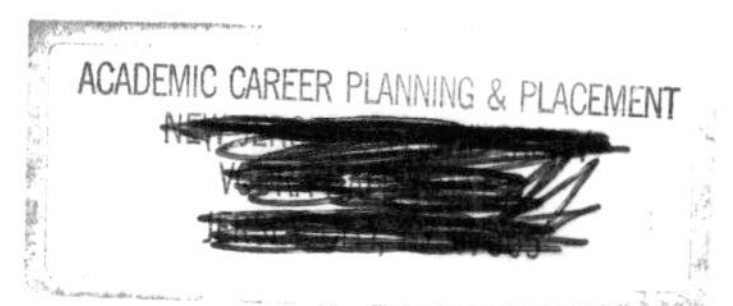

Killer Consulting Resumes!

2nd Edition

WetFeet, Inc.

The Folger Building
101 Howard Street, Suite 300
San Francisco, CA 94105
Phone: (415) 284-7900 or 1-800-926-4JOB
Fax: (415) 284-7910
Website: www.WetFeet.com

Killer Consulting Resumes!

2nd Edition
ISBN: 1-58207-460-7

Table of Contents

Consulting Resumes at a Glance

The Resume's Raison d'Etre

- 30 seconds or less to get you to the interview room—or not
- Guide for subsequent discussion in your interview
- Will NOT get you a job

Cover Letters

- Do not play a major role
- Could get you disqualified from consideration

Anatomy of the Resume

- Content: Education, Experience, Other
- Format: think clean, clear, conservative
- Avoid: Career Objective, skills resumes, colored paper

The Big Four Characteristics Sought by Consultants

- Analytical ability
- Intellect
- Leadership potential
- Achievement/results

Telling Your Story

Think about things you've done that demonstrate the Big Four—remember, it doesn't have to have been in a consulting context.

Overview

You're dying to get an interview with Monitor, McKinsey, Mercer. The deadline to submit your materials is only days away. You know that hundreds of your classmates are applying to get a spot on the same crowded interview schedule. Palatino, Times, Helvetica—bold, italic—nothing seems to make your resume look any better. Worse, you know there's no way you'll be able to add another extracurricular presidency to your list of "Other Activities" by next week. Even you aren't convinced that your resume is worth a second look. You start thinking about how to allocate your bid points and get not just one but several interviews with top firms. It's a mathematical impossibility.

Well, maybe. But maybe not.

There's no question that competition for jobs with the elite management consulting firms is fierce. At leading business schools, at least 75 percent of students interview with some of the big firms. However, it is not true that consulting firms hire only people with 4.0 GPAs. Nor do they hire only people with consulting experience. All the leading firms want to attract new blood. And they compete intensely with each other to hire top candidates. If you really are interested in a consulting job, you might as well be one of those under consideration.

In most cases, the first step along this path is to land an interview. And to land a consulting interview you must have a resume—and it will need to be good. Your resume must convincingly present your consulting skills and capabilities. And this is possible regardless of whether you've already been a consultant. By identifying and presenting your analytical, intellectual, and leadership capabilities in a form that consultants can easily understand, you'll undoubtedly improve

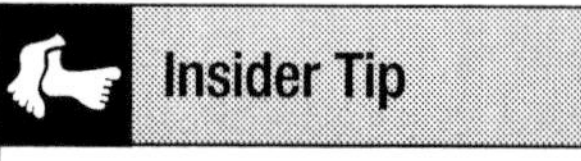

As any good marketer knows, packaging is often as important as content.

your chances of at least finding your way into the interview process.

This Insider Guide is designed to help you do the best possible job of presenting your qualifications for a consulting position. Although it won't land you a job at a prestigious firm—there's a lot more to getting a job offer than sending in a resume—it should give you insight into how the resume review process works and what firms are seeking. At the very least it should help you avoid the cardinal sin of selling yourself short. While there are countless resume-writing guides on the market, we have yet to discover any that are geared specifically toward management consulting. This publication is an exception. It is designed to help college and graduate students (or anyone else pondering a career in consulting) present themselves effectively to recruiters, resume readers, and interviewers from the top management consulting firms in the United States.

We interviewed insiders from ten of the industry's elite firms (including McKinsey, Bain, Booz Allen, and Accenture) to find out exactly what they look for in resumes, cover letters, and—down the line—interviews. Although there was some variation, the comments were remarkably consistent: As any good marketer knows, packaging is often as important as content. In this Insider Guide, we show you how to get a handle on both as you prepare to write your resume. We start by looking at how firms view resumes (and cover letters). We continue with a description of the standard consulting resume and suggestions about structure and format, after which we tell you how to turn your experiences and education into something that will appeal to the consulting resume reviewer. Then we provide reviews of real resumes, along with suggestions for improvement. We conclude with a discussion of how to move from the resume to the interview room. After that, it's up to you.

Are you ready to begin? Let's dive in!

The Bottom Line

Remember this: Your resume will *not* get you a consulting job. However it is essential to getting your foot in the door of a top firm and putting your candidacy into serious consideration. On average, the resume readers we interviewed spend 30 seconds reviewing a resume the first time. In 30 seconds an excellent resume conveys an image of who you are, what you're capable of, and how you have used your capabilities to accomplish results. It indicates that you know yourself well and have a firm grasp of what you bring to the consulting table.

Although insiders tell us that "there isn't one right answer" to the question of how to create a good resume (good news for most of us!), they say the best resumes are concise, results-oriented, and very clearly presented. The correct structure can make you a more likely interview target and can even help you sail more smoothly through the interview process. Through conversations with insiders and reviews of resume books, we found that a lot of aspiring consultants don't understand this. We hope this guide will help you get ahead of them in line.

Firm's-Eye View

How Cover Letters Are Used

Whereas your resume will almost always accompany you through the interview process, the cover letter is less important to your candidacy. Sometimes it is attached to the resume when it's forwarded, sometimes not.

Insiders overwhelmingly indicated that little, if any, attention is paid to cover letters. Sometimes they're read, sometimes not. Because of this, a cover letter is almost more of a courtesy than a necessity (though we would not advise submitting a resume through the mail without attaching a cover letter). Those who do read cover letters say they are useful to introduce a resume, highlight a few relevant points, and explain why the person is interested in interviewing with a particular firm. It seems cover letters are like standardized test scores: a bad one (or lack of one) can hurt you, but a good one won't necessarily help you. No recruiter we spoke with could recall outstanding or memorable points mentioned in a candidate's cover letter.

That said, there are a few cases in which cover letters are more important than indicated above. They are definitely more important when you send your resume to a firm directly, instead of through a campus recruiting program. In such a case the recipient might benefit from a brief introduction to you before scanning your resume. Insiders also tell us that cover letters are used to assess candidates' ability to write clearly and concisely. For example, candidates with a strong technical focus who might not be skilled writers and international candidates whose first language is not English but who are seeking a position in the United States undergo such scrutiny. When recruiters review resumes from career changers looking to make a switch from industry to consulting, they often look to the cover letter to understand the candidate's interest in consulting and for evidence of compelling skills that are readily transferable from the candidate's prior experience.

How Resumes Are Used

Having been intimately involved with your word-processing software over the last several days, you have a pretty good understanding of what it takes to produce a resume. But what happens to it after it leaves your hands? Our consulting insiders tell us that your resume and cover letter have an important but limited role in the selection and evaluation process.

From the firm's point of view, the resume has one primary purpose: to help determine which candidates merit interviews. No more, no less. A well-executed resume will increase your chances of getting an interview. It won't get you a job offer. Secondarily, your resume will often serve as the basis for ongoing evaluation of your candidacy. Each person who interviews you will probably have a copy of your resume. Often the interviewer will also have a copy of the comments of those who have already interviewed you. Your interviewer is likely to use the resume to identify areas to explore during the interview. Weaknesses or holes will be probed, strengths will be questioned, and anything that seems suspect will definitely be tested.

Insiders stress that although the resume is just one piece of the puzzle, it is a very important piece, for it is often the first impression you will make on a firm and on those who will meet you for an interview. You owe it to yourself to put your best foot forward.

Most firms recruit regionally and have recruiting teams in each of their offices or regions to cover one or more schools. Recruiting teams are usually made up of consultants from several levels (ranging from undergrad hires to partners or

VPs) as well as one or more administrative support staffers. At least one of the recruiters will probably be a recent graduate of your school. This helps the recruiting teams distinguish real and inflated points on a resume and make informed judgments of your credentials. For example, at one school, being on the Dean's list might mean you're in the top half of your class, while at another, that distinction is reserved for only the top few students. Such differences are important and will be noted as your resume is reviewed. As one insider puts it, "We know what's what on the resumes."

Consultants responsible for recruiting are usually busy juggling client work, practice-development work, and several other projects. They tend to review hundreds of resumes at a time and have very little time to spend on each one.

Your resume will likely be read by at least two consultants on the team who are appointed to review independently submitted resumes and resume books from target schools. These consultants select resumes that look promising based not only on the firm's criteria but also on their own judgment. We found no evidence of official resume grading systems at many firms, but most reviewers do keep a mental tally of so-called points or checks for each criterion the candidate appears to meet on his or her resume.

The next step at many firms is for the recruiting team to discuss the top candidates and decide who will receive interview offers. In these sessions the reviewer might be asked to describe the candidate, tell his or her "story," and explain what is compelling about the candidate. In some cases, a senior consultant will do a final resume review and make interview decisions, either after the group discussion or in lieu of it.

Remember, consultants responsible for recruiting are usually busy juggling client work, practice-development work, and several other projects. They tend to review hundreds of resumes at a time and have very little time to spend on each one. Knowing this will help you understand just how forgettable any single resume can be—and just how compelling yours must be to stand out.

Cover Letters Covered

In consulting recruiting, the cover letter is a little like the weather—it's taken for granted unless there's a problem. With that in mind, we recommend a low-risk strategy. The cover letter should be concise, well written, and at least somewhat personalized (enough so that the recruiter won't suspect that you've sent this same cover letter to multiple recipients, changing only the names of the recruiter and the company). Well-written cover letters establish a rapport with the reader and convey an image of professionalism, interest, and enthusiasm.

While the cover letter (or cover message if you're e-mailing) should be both thoughtful and personalized, this is not the place to regurgitate your resume in prose, nor is it the forum to explain the genesis of every academic or professional decision you've made to date. The purpose of the cover letter is to set the stage for your resume, not to explain anything on it—or worse, repeat it.

At a minimum, your cover letter should indicate the position to which you're applying, the primary reason for your interest in the specific role at the company, and a brief overview of the one or two qualifications that make you a compelling candidate. Finally, the cover letter should suggest logical next steps (politely, and never presumptuously), typically a brief telephone conversation or an in-person meeting. By the time you've covered each of these points, you'll probably have reached the desired cover letter length: no more than one page in hard copy, and no more than one screen shot if you're sending your resume via e-mail. If your message is polite, brief, well informed, and error-free, it will have served its primary purpose.

Follow the guidelines here to ensure that your cover letter covers all your bases.

Namedrop

Address the cover message to a particular person by name, and indicate how you have obtained that person's contact information. If you have learned of the position through a referral, mention the individual's name early in the e-mail; when a recruiter scans a cover message, he's more likely to pause and review your credentials if he recognizes a colleague's name in the text. Among two or more equally qualified candidates, most employers will prefer the candidate who came into the organization via a referral from an existing employee over someone who responded blindly to an ad on a job posting website or (worse) through an unsolicited resume.

Do Your Due Diligence

Before writing a cover letter to a firm, you should do some research on the firm. Identify what about that organization specifically interests you. It may be an industry or functional practice specialty, an article published by one of the firm's consultants, or a discussion with a current employee that generated your interest in the company. It helps if the reasons you cite for your interest don't belie blatant plagiarism of the company's website or word-for-word regurgitation of the job description; a little judicious paraphrasing never hurt anyone, but the obvious cut and paste ranks high among recruiters' lists of pet peeves.

Whatever the case, make sure that what you write is accurate and shows that you've done your homework. If you target BCG for its leadership in reengineering or Monitor for its 80-year history, you'll never make it into the reception area. You may want to purchase our detailed Insider Guides on specific top-tier firms or one of consulting guides. You can find a list of current titles on the last 2 pages of this Insider Guide.

Answer the Question, "What's in It for Me?"

The purpose of the cover letter is to communicate to the employer a specific personal message about your potential value to that organization. While you should include information on what specific factors have attracted you to the company, make sure your approach is balanced and describes why the *company* should be attracted to *you*. After all, your cover letter should suggest that hiring you would be a mutually beneficial decision for you and the employer. Don't just talk about what the company can do for you: Explain what skills and qualifications make you a compelling candidate.

Spotlight Your Strengths

The cover letter should include the reason you are interested in the firm and the highlights of your resume that make you a good candidate for that firm. If you have a nonbusiness background or are changing careers, you might briefly explain why you are pursuing a career in consulting. If you have a contact at the firm, mention that person. Better yet, send the resume directly to your contact to forward to the recruiter.

E-Mail Takes Cover, Too

Put the same care into preparing your cover letter when submitting your resume via e-mail. The ease and informality of e-mail can be deceptive and dangerous. Your e-mail cover letter serves the same purpose as the hard-copy version. No matter how brief your cover message, it has to be flawless. One insider recommends that candidates complete the "To:" field last as they prepare a cover message to introduce an e-mailed resume. This way, you're covered if you accidentally click "Send" before your message is ready. (This also applies to any "CC:" addressees.) Many people learn this rule only through a painful experience. "Ignore last message!" and "Oops!" e-mails are ineffective and can destroy your credibility.

Don't Be Presumptuous

Let's paint a picture for you. It's 10 a.m. on a Friday and the leader of your University's recruiting team—who just happens to be a consultant himself—opens his e-mail inbox to find your cover letter and resume. He's cranky—he's been on the road since Sunday night and didn't get to bed until 3 a.m. because of delays at LaGuardia. He's counting on an easy day at the office so that he can leave early and spend some quality time kicking a soccer ball around in the backyard with Junior. He can smell the aroma of freshly cut grass when he reads the end of your cover message: "I will call your office at 4 p.m. on Friday to arrange a convenient time for a telephone interview." He thinks to himself, "Who does this kid thinks he is?" You could be Michael Porter himself, and your resume might very well win a one-way ticket to the deleted items folder.

We're all about suggesting next steps in your cover letter, but don't assume that you're assured an interview or that you can elbow your way onto the recruiter's calendar at a time that's convenient for you. In your cover letter, it's much more diplomatic to request (politely, we might add) a brief telephone conversation or an in-person meeting rather than an interview. Furthermore, the stated purpose of this meeting should be to learn more about the firm, the position, or how the recruiter himself attained consulting fame and fortune through his raw intellectual horsepower and business acumen—not how he can help you land a job.

Anatomy of a Resume

The first step in preparing your resume is to understand (and accept) the basic rules, so that your presentation won't get you thrown out of the game. There are two areas in which you should conform to standard practice: packaging and content. Resume readers prefer to focus more on content, but it is format that enables them to pick out useful information quickly. To assure a good read, both content and format must be in tip-top shape. We discuss each in greater detail below, but as a general rule, these are not places to push the envelope. Remember, resume readers work 60-hour weeks solving problems for Fortune 500 companies. Few of them will give you extra credit for using bright blue paper or putting cartoons on your resume.

Resume Content

You need to customize your resume for consulting. If you are considering several types of consulting firms, you may even want to customize it according to the type of work the firm does, for example strategy vs. operations vs. technology (see WetFeet's online consulting firm profiles at www.WetFeet.com). We know that many candidates use the same resume for all inquiries, with a customized cover letter. If you do this you risk looking amorphous, like a politician trying to appeal to a broad constituency. Don't fall into this trap. If you really want that consulting interview, take time to write a solid resume that's relevant to the type of consulting work you are pursuing.

The most important thing to do when writing your resume is to be concise. One firm's vice president tells us, "If you can't reduce your resume to 1 page, I immediately think you are unable to tell the important from the trivial, which is a death sentence for a consultant."

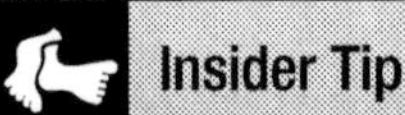

Resume readers prefer to focus more on content, but it is format that enables them to pick out useful information quickly.

Your consulting resume should have two sections: "Education" and "Experience." An "Other" section may be included if you have useful information that doesn't fit neatly into "Education" or "Experience." As for the sequence, you should lead with your strength. If you are a student, and particularly if you are from a top-ranked school, you should lead with "Education" unless you have outstanding experience that will better distinguish you. Experienced professionals (those a few years or more out of school) should always lead with and emphasize "Experience." As your school days become more distant, they become less relevant and firms become more interested in your professional experience than in the fact that you were editor of your school newspaper. The "Other" section should always be last.

Some resumes include "Career Objective," "Career Summary," or another general overview section. This information is superfluous. If you think you need to summarize your resume you have missed the mark. Remember, the resume itself is a summary of your experience, skills, and accomplishments. As for the "Career Objective," this information should be included in your cover letter. It is also self-evident: If you have sent your resume to a firm for consideration, surely you're looking for a job with that firm. The space would be better used to describe your considerable assets.

Education

This section might be more aptly titled "Education and Academic Achievement." Information here should include schools attended, degrees conferred and when, and other information regarding your academic achievement, including GPA, SAT/GRE/GMAT scores, scholarships and awards earned, honor society memberships, class ranking, and so on. List only those things that showcase your strengths. A 3.5 GPA isn't likely to impress anyone, nor is a 600 on the GMAT. These are perfectly respectable statistics, but they aren't going to wow the reader, so you might as well save the space for other details.

Coming from a top-ranked school is helpful, but it will hardly qualify you as unique at any of the best firms. One insider says, "If you're not from a brand-name school, most firms expect you to be in the top of the class." Another says, "The first thing that will cause me to throw out a resume is a second-rate school." When pressed, this insider defined a second-rate school as one not within the "top 20," which fortunately paves a fairly wide path among graduate schools. While there is more leeway in the college ranks, the "top school" sentiment is echoed at most major firms as a quick and easy way to separate the wheat from the chaff. If you're from a less well-known institution, whether it's a college or a graduate school, be prepared to show your strengths in other critical areas because your resume is likely to be a tougher sell.

Strong regional graduate schools are an exception to this philosophy. Since most firms recruit regionally, there is a good chance they'll go to a good local school if they have an office in the area, particularly if alums from the school work in that firm.

Experience

"The section on work experience should be short on description and long on verifiable results," says one insider. We couldn't agree more. Think of this as the results section, rather than the experience section, of your resume. You should certainly mention the type of work you've done and the industries in which you have experience, but all in the context of what you've accomplished. If you can quantify the results of your work, you'll be better off. This makes sense when you think of the type of work consultants do. The best firms can point to the direct impact that their work has on their clients' bottom lines (those that can't don't survive long!).

“ ”

The section on work experience should be short on description and long on verifiable results.

To do this, they use measurement systems that enable them and their clients to track progress along the way. They want you to have done the same for yourself and your career.

Consultants also care about the companies you've worked for. Companies that are known to have good training programs, such as General Electric or Procter & Gamble, play well. In addition, companies that have notoriously rigorous selection processes, such as certain investment banks or high-tech firms, score big points. A measure of success at any of these companies is a plus, because performing well for them indicates to the resume reader that you have what it takes to survive in a competitive, rigorous environment of well-qualified peers.

If your experience is in a nontraditional business area, such as the public sector, nonprofit, or other nonbusiness, you're going to have a tougher time. "I tend to shy away from goofy backgrounds such as Mother Teresa's nuns, Peace Corps, or other areas with no direct business experience," says one consultant. "My assumption," says another, "is that they can't add value to the client if they don't know how business works, and we really don't want to bill the clients to give these people their first business experience." Others said unusual backgrounds were fine, as long as they revealed a record of accomplishment. "I remember the resume of a person with an art-history major who had taken initiative and started some programs at her school," one recruiter said. "Although she didn't have a traditional background, her experience showed results." Suffice it to say that if your background isn't obviously business-related you'll need to be much more specific about the results you have attained, and be clear about how such achievements will enable you to excel as a consultant.

If you have a nontraditional background, you should also keep in mind that individual firms have different levels of tolerance for and interest in attracting people from diverse backgrounds. To that end, you'll want to be sure to do your homework on each firm's hiring practices.

> “ ”
>
> **One woman actually wrote on her resume that her favorite ice cream flavor was chocolate. She was probably trying to be cute and attract attention, but we definitely don't need those types on our team.**

Other (or: Activities, Additional Information, Personal)

This section is your opportunity to tell the scanner a little more about yourself. Details typically include activities, interests, associations, memberships, and skills not already covered, such as proficiency in foreign languages. Such areas of your life may be relevant to how you will perform as a consultant—and relevance is the key. Remember, consulting isn't only about crunching numbers and creating great PowerPoint presentations. You need strong communication skills and the ability to tolerate various personalities, ambiguity, and so on. For more of what appeals to consultants, see "Looking for Ms. or Mr. Right."

You can also use the "Other" section to mention activities that hint at gender, race, religion, sexual orientation, and so on. Honestly, you may have a slight advantage if your activities indicate that you fall into a group that the company is trying to recruit. This is a touchy subject, but many firms are desperate to recruit a varied workforce to serve an increasingly diverse clientele. We constantly hear complaints from recruiters about how difficult it is to find diverse candidates. Therefore, highlighting your diversity could help your candidacy.

At the same time, involvement in activities that could be viewed as controversial could spell trouble. If you've championed your fervent political or religious beliefs by leading campus protests or abortion rights marches, for example, you may want to tone down (or omit) descriptions of these pursuits from your resume. While you may feel passionately about these activities, remember that consulting firms prioritize your perceived cultural fit with the organization when they're making hiring decisions. At the resume review stage, you don't want to raise red flags that you might be a cultural mismatch at the firm by describing your politically charged or potentially controversial activities early in the process.

On the other hand, insiders tell us that interesting or unusual information in this section can play a significant role in the decision to award an interview. "I saw a woman's resume with a blurb at the bottom on how she started an organization to educate the homeless in her city, and I thought, this is someone who identifies problems and takes initiative to solve them. This is the type of person we need on our projects," says one consultant. However, we caution against using this section for frivolous information. Many people we interviewed said they had rejected otherwise decent resumes because of strange mentions in the "Other" section. "One woman actually wrote on her resume that her favorite ice cream flavor was chocolate," a reviewer recalls. "She was probably trying to be cute and attract attention, but we definitely don't need those types on our team. I felt no guilt in dinging her."

While it probably won't elicit such a strong reaction, including personal interests that are fairly common (cooking, travel, jogging, and reading, e.g.) probably won't win you any points because they appear in resumes so frequently. Lines like "traveled extensively through Europe" almost never achieve their desired effect for the same reason. By no means would we suggest that you omit these perfectly legitimate hobbies and experiences from your "Other" section, but if you're trying to choose which items to include in this section, include the ones that are most likely to pique the genuine interest of the recruiter.

Resume Format

> “ ”
>
> **I'm always suspicious when I see a skills-based resume. I feel like I have to make a leap of faith.**

Consultants are sticklers about presentation. Almost any consultant who has drawn a slide can tell you a story about the time a client pointed out a typo in a slide and used that as a basis for criticizing several months' worth of solid research. With that in mind, stick with a format that's error-free, clean, and easy to read and that clearly shows the two main sections: “Education” and “Experience.” Anything fancy is at best irrelevant, at worst a negative factor that can result in a rejection letter. Remember, the format of your resume has one objective: to make your qualifications easy to understand.

Conform to the Norm

Conforming to standard resume format is generally considered a good thing. One recruiting head tells us, “I like the basic sections: ‘Education,’ ‘Experience,’ ‘Interest.’ Dates on the left, body of text with bullet points, starting with verbs, all the same tense. To the right of the company name, I like to see the location of the company for which someone worked because I want to make sure they're interested in living/working here.”

A Word About Skills

Many resume books discuss the virtues of the skills-based resume format for dressing up your experience, especially when you've had many positions or are trying to change careers. We have one word about skills resumes: Fuggedabowdit! None of our insiders like this alternative format. “I'm always suspicious when I see a skills-based resume,” one tells us. “I feel like I have to make a leap of faith. I prefer to see experience that illustrates skills I'm looking for.” Another consultant is more direct. “I hate reading skills resumes,” he says. “Sometimes I don't bother.”

A Note to Those with Technical and Scientific Backgrounds

With the market for e-business and IT consulting booming, many firms are likely to have a better understanding of the type of work involved in scientific research and development and will probably have consultants with similar backgrounds screen technical resumes. This is good news for you science PhDs hoping to break into consulting. It means your stellar research accomplishments won't go unnoticed, and you might not have to explain the significance of your discovery of microsecond time lags in X-ray binaries. It also means that your resume, if written in a non-standard format, may be comprehensible to at least a few reviewers. But why risk it? If your background appears focused in science and technology, however, be prepared for quizzing about your people skills: leadership, teamwork, communication.

Formatting Guidelines for Resumes and Cover Letters

While most resume reviewers don't have a specific model in mind, all seem to appreciate consistency. This generally means the following:

- A single, standard font: Times, Helvetica, or similar
- A readable font size: 11- or 12-point preferred, but no smaller than 10
- Neutral paper color: white or off-white
- Standard layout: 1-inch margins (or more), left justified, line spaces between sections
- Clear resume organization: two or three sections labeled clearly, chronological listing with dates on the left, bulleted points
- Clear letter organization: business format with one or two paragraphs, addressee name, company name, and date at the top

This also means you should resist the temptation to use excessive text formatting, graphics, or a matrix or graph. Such extras eat up space that could be dedicated to providing evidence of your qualifications, getting you additional checks or points, and helping you to land in the "call back" pile. Remember, cuteness may be perceived as desperation. One insider tells us he's suspicious of resumes and cover letters that use attention-grabbing tactics. "Why are they so worried their qualifications won't stand out?" he asks.

You may want to use bullets. Why?

- Bullets make your resume more concise.
- Bullets make your resume easier to scan.
- Consultants love bullets; they write in bullets; they even think in bullets.

Insiders tell us that consultants are more likely to toss a resume into the ding pile than to spend extra time plowing through turgid, clunky prose to find what they're looking for. "I'm impressed when someone has enough confidence to write just one line followed by short bullet points," one partner tells us. "I know writers can bullshit their way through things by writing prose," comments another.

When you write bullets, remember the following:

- Keep them short (one line if possible).
- Start them with action verbs.
- Make them consistent.

(Note: Consultants love horizontal page layouts, too, but we don't recommend that format for resumes yet.)

E-Mail and Online Submissions

Once you've crafted the perfect resume, be sure to save it in three electronic versions:

1. Microsoft Word or other word-processing software document: This is your presentation resume—the one with every formatting and stylistic bell and whistle printed on good quality, heavy bond paper. This is the one that you'll send to recruiters via regular mail and the one you'll take with you when you interview. Keep several copies on hand.

2. ASCII format with line breaks: ASCII (American Standard Code of Interchange) allows databases and data recognition software to read your resume without the confusion caused by formatting. Use this version to cut and paste your document into the body of an e-mail message. In Microsoft Word, use the "Save as" option to save your resume (named differently from the first version) as plain text. Select the "Insert line breaks" checkbox.

3. ASCII format without line breaks: Use this to upload your resume to an online database and to cut and paste into preset fields. Follow the directions for number 2 above, but skip the last step.

Using ASCII versions will help you avoid formatting conflicts that can make your document difficult to read. Unfortunately, in the ASCII versions you will also lose the formatting you took great care to develop. To minimize the damage:

1. Replace bullets with asterisks (*).

2. Offset category headings with a row of tildes (~) or capital letters.

3. Change your margin settings to 2 inches; 60 characters (including spaces) is the maximum line length. Setting a wider margin allows you to control where the line breaks occur.

4. Select a fixed-width typeface like Courier and a 12-point font size.

5. Add white space for readability.

6. Do a test run. E-mail your resume to yourself or a friend to see how it looks.

E-Mailed Resumes

In recent years, the prevalence of both spam and computer viruses has changed the rules of the road for communicating with potential employers via e-mail. In an effort to combat spam (which reportedly constitutes a whopping 60 percent of all e-mail traffic), many companies use sophisticated spam filters to guard inboxes from suspicious e-mails. Typically, these filters simply delete suspected spam or divert it into folders that automatically dump e-mails after they go unchecked for a certain period of time. You might be wondering how this phenomenon affects you, the innocent jobseeker who's simply trying to apply for a job at a consulting firm. After all, you're not peddling Viagra or body part enlargement products, so your e-mailed resume should be safe, right?

Wrong. As it turns out, following the very suggestions intended to get your resume noticed by those people in a position to hire you may run afoul of spam filter technology. For example, most trusted career counselors (including us!) advise job seekers to quantify the results of their work (preferably in dollars and cents) wherever possible. After all, who could deny that the phrase "increased sales by over $50,000,000" would catch a recruiter's eye? As it turns out, phrases like these may instead catch the attention of spam filter technology, which can't differentiate between "Increased sales by $1,000,000," and "Work at home; make $10,000 a month."

Likewise, one job seeker sent his resume to a consumer products company, proudly highlighting the fact that he had graduated from his MBA program *magna cum laude*. He received an automated response alerting him that his e-mail had been deleted because it contained a supposed obscenity. He changed "magna cum laude" to "with high honors," resubmitted his resume, and received an automated reply thanking him for his interest in the company. It turns out this jobseeker was one of the lucky ones; most spam filters won't let you know which specific work they find troublesome; in fact, many won't generate an automated e-mail letting you know that your resume has been trashed.

E-Mailed Resumes (cont'd)

The spam filter will simply delete the "offensive" e-mail, relegating your resume to a virtual black hole among advertisements for erectile dysfunction remedies and black market prescription drugs.

How can you avoid the curse of the overzealous spam filter? We've provided the following checklist to help you out:

First and foremost, follow directions!

If a company has advised you not to send e-mail attachments, don't do it. In fact, unless a company or recruiter has *specifically* instructed you to send your resume as an attachment, you should send it in the body of your e-mail in plain text format. Because computer viruses are a major threat, most recipients prefer that you include your resume directly in the body of your e-mail. In other cases, their servers may automatically delete attachments as a security measure. And if you've blatantly ignored the company's instructions by sending an e-mail attachment when they wanted a plain text resume in the body of the e-mail, then you've simply given them an easy ding.

We know that resumes e-mailed in plain text won't win any beauty contests, but they represent the most reliable way to communicate your qualifications to hiring personnel. If you simply can't bear the thought of sending a plain text resume on its own, you can always follow up with a properly formatted and stylized paper copy in the mail—provided, of course, that you know the name of the specific person to whom you're supposed to send it. If the envelope is simply addressed to "Human Resources" or "Personnel," you can be sure that your pretty bond paper resume will never see the light of day.

Two words: easy access.

If you have been instructed to send your resume as an attachment, make sure it's in Microsoft Word (or a comparable basic software package) and include your name (at

E-Mailed Resumes (cont'd)

least your last name) in the name of the file (Jane_Doe_resume.doc) so that it can be reunited with your cover message if the two part ways. Unless specifically instructed to do so, don't send it as a compressed file or as a PDF. Trust us: If the recipient can't open your file successfully the first time around, she's not going to chase you down to request a more compatible file.

One more tip for resumes and cover letters attached to e-mails: When you run spell-check before sending off your attachments, make sure to click on "Ignore All" for any words, terms, or proper names that your spell check doesn't recognize. You don't want the recruiter to open up a resume and cover letter filled with red and green squiggly lines.

Choose a spam filter-resistant subject line.

Don't leave the subject line blank, but do keep it short and sweet. Avoid words in the subject line that are often used by spammers, such as "free," "offer," "increase," and so on. In short, the less your e-mail looks like a spam message, the less likely it will be filtered. If you're responding to an online job announcement, you may want to include the job title or requisition number in the subject line, keeping in mind that the recruiter receiving your message may be responsible for filling multiple positions. The job posting will often include specific instructions for what to include in the subject line; these aren't suggestions—make sure that you follow the directions that the employer has outlined.

Leave punctuation marks (especially exclamation marks) out of the subject line, and don't use all capital letters or colored backgrounds. While it may be tempting to use the subject line of an e-mail as a marketing ploy to grab a recruiter's attention—Attention! Ace Analyst Available—we recommend a more conservative approach that will help the person on the receiving end track, file, or forward your resume to an interested colleague. When in doubt, include your name and the position applied for. For example:

E-Mailed Resumes (cont'd)

- Grace Adler, Business Analyst
- Karen Walker, MBA

Check your resume itself for words that are overused in spam.

If you're like the vast majority of the population, you probably have an informed frame of reference on this one. (When in doubt, pay attention to the types of e-mail that your own spam filter weeds out.) When you're thinking of the action phrases that most aptly describe your achievements, stay away from ones that are also used to market unsavory content over e-mail. In other words, you may not wish to say that you've "enhanced" or "enlarged" anything, even if these terms are used in a perfectly appropriate way in your resume. Thanks to spammers, even innocent words like "free," "expand," "trial," "mortgage," and "increased," and phrases like "rapid growth" might be misconstrued by a spam filter. We're not suggesting that you omit these terms entirely from your resume, but forewarned is forearmed: Take a good look at your resume, consider the phrases that might trigger a spam filter into action, and tweak the language where you can. For example, rather than citing the $50,000,000 in sales you've personally supervised, change your numerical reference to $50 million, which is less likely to set off the spam filter alarm bells. (We know it's sad, but such is the world we live in today.)

Whatever the context, omit the word "spam" itself from your correspondence (i.e., "I'm writing to make sure that you received my resume, which may have been diverted to a spam folder in your inbox.")

Choose a professional e-mail address for your job search.

Stay away from clever, cutesy or—even worse—potentially provocative e-mail addresses. You may think that nachomama@whatever.com is absolutely hilarious, but neither the recruiter nor the company's spam filter is likely to find your wit endearing. (We should

 **E-Mailed Resumes (cont'd)**

point out that even if spam filters weren't an issue, we still wouldn't think e-mail addresses like these were a good idea. Few consultants would hire a "nachomama" anyway.) In addition, some experts suggest that you avoid numbers in your e-mail address to the left of the @ symbol. Even if you use something as innocuous as your birthday or anniversary as the tag line (janedoe42801@whatever.com), it looks like it may contain the tracking code that some spammers use. Err on the side of caution and change your e-mail address to one that has few or no numbers in it.

Send your e-mails in plain text—not HMTL—format.

How can you tell which is which? If you're writing an e-mail in which you can alter the appearance of text (you can italicize, underline, or you can change the font), then you're not sending it in plain text. Some e-mail providers only allow users to write in plain text; if you want to double check and you're using Microsoft Outlook, click "format" in your new message window and be sure that "plain text" is the selected format.

Play it safe.

If you have a personal contact within the organization to which you are applying, consider asking her to forward your resume to the appropriate hiring manager on your behalf. (Not only does this increase the odds that you'll defeat the spam filter, but internal referrals typically boost your overall credibility as a candidate.) If that's not an option, run every version of your resume and cover letter through a few different spam filters before you send them to a potential employer. If you can, follow up on your e-mailed resume with a hard copy sent through the regular mail. Not only will you ensure that your resume has reached its destination, but you can include a more attractive Microsoft Word version with your desired formatting.

Top Ten Things Interviewers Look for When Reviewing a Resume

10. The time zone you live in.
9. Something that makes you stand out from all the other Stanford/Harvard/Wharton graduates applying for this job.
8. A balance (as if consultants really know what that means!).
7. Experience in the industry of his current client and availability to be staffed immediately.
6. A typo—so he can throw it out.
5. Evidence that you'll be willing to jump on a plane and spend every week in Tacoma (without complaining).
4. Someone who went to her alma mater. Not that she's biased.
3. An indication that the person is breathing.
2. "I'll know it when I see it."
1. "You're assuming I actually get a chance to read resumes."

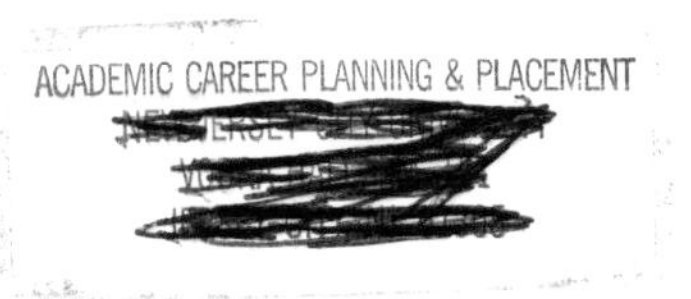

Study Break

Consulting firms just love to tout their differences. And we all know that the primary factors differentiating firms are their people. We've researched what several of the top firms seek in their candidates to get an idea of the real differences among them. Crack the WetFeet Consulting Candidate–Babble Challenge by matching each firm to its ideal candidates. (Answers following table.)

Looking for Ms. and Mr. Right

Firm	Ideal Candidates
Towers Perrin **McKinsey & Co.** **Booz Allen Hamilton** **Marakon Associates** **Bain & Co.** **Monitor Co.** **Deloitte Consulting** **A.T. Kearney**	1. "We look for adaptability, variety, and leadership. If you've only worked at a paint store, then tell us how you moved up from sweeping the floors to custom-color mixer to regional manager." 2. "Individuals with comparatively strong records of academic and managerial or professional achievement who have the capacity for continuous development." 3. "Highly motivated individuals who possess excellent analytical and interpersonal abilities, a keen business sense, proven leadership skills, and a strong academic record." 4. "Confident, outgoing people with a sustained record of achievement, quantitative aptitude, strong interpersonal skills, and—most important—a willingness, even eagerness, to

Looking for Ms. and Mr. Right (cont'd)

Ideal Candidates

solve problems and make change happen out in the frontier of new ideas, new managerial approaches, new modes of analysis, and new geographies."

5. "Individuals who are exceptional performers, have innate curiosity and enthusiasm, and tremendous capacity for providing insight, building solutions and providing value for our clients from start to finish."

6. "Candidates with the potential to grow into outstanding client, team and firm leaders. . . . we focus on core capabilities such as integrity, intellectual curiosity, initiative and interpersonal skills."

7. "Individuals who have demonstrated high academic achievement and strong analytical, communication, and problem-solving skills, along with a creative ability and deep commitment to the firm's values."

8. "We look for not only strong generalists, we also look for people who have good functional expertise."

Answers: 1) Deloitte Consulting; 2) McKinsey; 3) Bain; 4) Monitor; 5) A.T. Kearney; 6) Marakon; 7) Towers Perrin; 8) Booz Allen.

The Consultant's Perspective

Each firm has its own strategy for navigating the resume flow—you'll want to do your homework on their respective businesses, cultures, and staffing approaches to get a sense of their priorities. Naturally, it makes sense to target firms that have an obvious need for people with your background. Within each organization, however, there are often several different breeds of resume reviewer. Based on our research, we've grouped them as three different species: general scanners, spike seekers, and idealists. You won't know which type will pick up your resume. However, as you figure out how to present your skills, it's useful to know how various consultants sort through their stacks.

Types of Resume Reviewers

General Scanners

General scanners have a broad list of attributes in mind and spend a minimal amount of time matching resumes to their criteria. One insider explains, "I start by doing a quick scan, looking for the obvious scoop on the person: Did they go to a top school? Have they worked for good companies? What functional knowledge do they have? It's really helpful if this information comes immediately to the eye. If I like what I see, then I'll read through the entire resume." This approach is fairly typical of the way a general scanner reads resumes. Another comments, "I try to get through a resume in under 30 seconds. If I find a possible candidate, I may spend up to 3 minutes trying to figure the person out—to really understand what the words mean, what they really did, what problems they really worked on, how much responsibility they really had."

Spike Seekers

Spike seekers love highlights. "I'm looking for the one thing that will make this person special in the office," one manager tells us. "It could be a blinding problem-solver or a person who keeps morale up. This should come out clearly in the resume." Several consultants told us they need to be able to tell a compelling story about the candidate, often a story about how one or two very strong and unique traits come through clearly in the resume.

Idealists

Some reviewers have an ideal in mind before they start reading, and look for how well a resume measures up against it. "I look for elements of the triad: leadership, academics (a 3.8 GPA or above and mention of honors), and a team-type activity such as sports or community involvement. Many are very strong in two of the three, but few have the perfect triad, which would be our ideal candidate." Other idealists have a preference for one thing they'd like to see on a resume, based on their own experience as well as their observations of how past hires have performed. These individuals are the most difficult to please, because they each look for different things. Others believe experience is a better indicator of a good consultant than either grades or test scores. "I always start with the experience," one tells us. "Most people went to a top school and earned good grades. Experience is what really differentiates the resumes. And it's the most important factor in finding successful candidates for our practice." Another reviewer says, "I look for progression of responsibility. Everyone presents themselves as having achieved an enormous amount, but it doesn't always tell a good story about how the person has grown."

Common Characteristics

Although we've identified some very specific methods of resume review, we found overwhelming similarity in what reviewers consider to be important resume attributes. Most look for three or four required elements and several others that point to a candidate's likely success as a consultant. As a general rule, candidates are not expected to excel in each of the required areas, but they should have checks in all of them and show outstanding capability in at least one. The Big Four most frequently identified "required" areas are as follows:

1. Analytical and problem-solving ability

2. Intellectual capacity

3. Leadership capability or potential

4. Aspiration, achievement, and a record of results

(We discuss these factors in greater depth and how you can demonstrate your skills in these areas in the following section.)

Additional important factors include the following:

- Relevant industry or functional experience (very important for experienced hires)
- Ability to work well on a team
- People skills—ability to communicate effectively
- Ability to balance multiple responsibilities
- Top schools
- Interesting activities
- Background of personal interest or relevance to the reader

Some of the above items aren't on an official resume review list, but they influence whether resumes are selected. Different firms weigh these items differently, depending on the type of work they do and how they deploy junior-level staff. BCG, for example, tends to emphasize raw intelligence, while CSC emphasizes relevant experience.

Preparing to Write

Know Thy Audience and Thyself

We can't stress enough the need to do your homework on the firms you are targeting. This information can help you think about what, specifically, might appeal to the recruiting team at your chosen firm, and it is most relevant should you choose to include a reference in the cover letter. Look into the firm's noted areas of strength and focus, find out which industry or functional practice areas it pursues and find out where the nearest office is. All of this information should influence the way in which you write your resume and cover letter, and especially the way in which you pursue an interview. Most firms have a website you can quickly check for some basic information.

Before you begin writing your resume you must also scrutinize yourself. Which elements of your years of wisdom, experience, and accomplishment belong on a single sheet of paper, and which don't? What characteristics make you stand out from the crowd but also show that you're a team player? This section will help you think through your activities and accomplishments and tell your compelling life story—in a way that interests consultants—in 1 page.

WetFeet Resume Tip

Resume reviewers look favorably on candidates with backgrounds similar to their own. Read the employee profiles included in most firms' recruiting materials and websites and find someone who worked in the same company or attended the same school you did. You'll have a better chance of getting a favorable review.

Collect Information about Yourself

In addition to knowing all the factual information about yourself—grades, test scores, and so on—you need to think about how to portray yourself in a positive, confident light while telling the true story of who you are and what you've accomplished. You must have a good deal of insight into your experience, strengths, and weaknesses to create a compelling resume. The sources of inspiration for this vary. The following are just a few.

Academic Records

Gather your school transcripts, standardized test scores, scholarship applications and awards, or any other information that may help you paint a picture of your academic capability. Calculate your GPA, because you'll probably need this information at some point. If you are concerned about your GPA, calculate it using several cuts—overall, major-only, by year, and so on—to see which provides the most favorable view to note on your resume or at least mention in the first interview. Also, be sure to use a standard 4.0 scale.

Recommendations

Re-read any recommendations written for you—for school, job, or contest applications. Make note of the strengths mentioned. You should highlight these strengths as you describe your experience and accomplishments in your resume.

Performance Reviews

Employer reviews may contain information on your rating vis-à-vis your peers. They may also include assessments of your accomplishments during your tenure. They are another good source of strengths and possibly of some quantitative results you've achieved in your career.

Employment History

If you don't already have one, prepare a chronological history of the major jobs you've held. Include the company names, your titles, your managers' names, the time you spent in those positions, your starting and ending salaries, and your primary responsibilities. This will be very useful in identifying upward trends in your career—increasing responsibility, increasing salary, or other advancement. Your employment history will also help you identify any gaps that will need to be accounted for on the resume or in the interview.

Employment History

Dates	Firm	Position	Responsibilities	Start Salary	End Salary

Review Your Top Accomplishments

List the most significant accomplishments from your professional, academic, and personal lives. Write down each accomplishment, explain why it is significant to you, how you achieved it, how others helped you, and how you measure its success. You will need to include information about at least two of your top accomplishments in your resume, preferably with an indication of the results achieved.

Survey Your Strengths

Using the information you've gathered, think about the types of work or activities in which you have consistently succeeded—those situations in which you've performed well and felt good about it. The skills you used in these situations are most likely some of your strengths. Include evidence of these on your resume so the reader can identify you as a strong analyst, born leader, or formidable writer. These areas will likely be explored further in your interviews and you'll need to have thought through some examples from your resume.

Consider Your Weaknesses

You obviously won't highlight your weaknesses on your resume, but omission of information might prompt an interviewer to question you about these areas. If your resume lacks information on leadership positions, for example, you will need to show strengths in several other areas. It's a good idea to have thought through this before your interview anyway, because some interviewers still ask the old "What are your weaknesses?" question.

Strengths & Weaknesses

Develop Your Spiel

Once you've written your resume, develop and practice a 20- to 30-second spiel that summarizes your experience and major achievements. You will use this countless times, to introduce yourself over the phone or in an interview when the interviewer has not had a chance to review your qualifications. This will also be your answer to the dangerously open-ended "Tell me about yourself" lead-in that so many interviewers open with. Preparing your spiel will help you articulate the items listed on your resume.

30-Second Spiel

You Can't Recreate Your Past, But You Can Reposition It

If you suspect that the only people who get consulting interviews are those who have already been consultants, you're partially correct. Certainly, many firms are biased toward experienced consultants who can "hit the ground running." And they are relatively safe in assuming that someone who has been a consultant before has the skills and characteristics required to do the work. However, consulting firms continually have to bring in new blood as well. (The turnover rate is much too high for firms to survive on industry veterans alone.) Therefore, if you haven't worked for a consulting firm in the past, you should try for the next best thing: demonstrating that you've done the same type of work, even if it was in a different context.

How can you do this if you've never consulted a day in your life? Well, first of all, you probably have done something that resembles consulting. Remember, consulting in its purest form is problem solving. Who hasn't had a chance to take a problem, analyze it, make hypotheses about it, and, through research, come to understand whether those hypotheses are correct? Examples of this could come from work, school, or extracurricular activities.

Second, as discussed above, your consulting resume reviewer will likely be looking for evidence of skills in several areas: analytical ability, intelligence, leadership capability, and so on. Think about the things you have done that will showcase your abilities in these areas. In the next sections, we review some of the attributes most frequently sought by insiders. Each section also includes a list of questions that will help you identify work you have performed or activities you have pursued that will demonstrate your consulting skills.

Analytical and Problem-Solving Ability

Analytical and problem-solving skills are critical components of a consulting resume. They are fundamental to your success as a consultant, especially during the first few years. If you show no evidence of these skills, you'd better be stellar in the other areas. Expect to have your problem-solving and analytic abilities tested in your interviews.

Have you

- Used spreadsheets to create data models?
- Synthesized large amounts of information to draw conclusions?
- Identified a problem and taken a proactive approach to solving it?
- Used an unexpected method or tactic to further progress?
- Identified a root cause from an array of symptoms and developed a solution?
- Performed experiments that required formulation of a hypothesis and collection of evidence to prove or disprove it?

If so, you may have the problem-solving ability firms look for. Be sure to mention these activities as part of your discussion of work experience or accomplishments.

Intellectual Achievement

Intellectual achievement is one thing consulting firms test for in case interviews. If you graduated from college magna cum laude with a technical degree, you might be safe. If not, expect a lot of scrutiny. It's hard to do much repackaging here. You either have it or you don't. But a lack of honors probably will not disqualify you from the running if you have attended rigorous schools, earned good grades, and scored well on tests.

Have you

- Earned honors or other academic awards?
- Received academic scholarships?
- Taken particularly challenging courses or had a heavy workload?
- Pursued intellectual activities (e.g., chess)?
- Attended academically rigorous schools?
- Aced your SATs or GMATs?
- Earned a high GPA (3.6 or higher, depending on the firm)?

If so, you'll receive points in the academic capacity category. That's important because academics is one of the more black-and-white categories and often one of the least flexible. Resume reviewers usually are not lenient in this area because a weak academic record could indicate either an inability to perform work or, simply, laziness.

Leadership Capability or Potential

Leadership, or the potential to lead, is at the top of most firms' wish lists. Firms always look for individuals who have risen to leadership positions on any team or in school organizations or companies.

Have you

- Managed people?
- Facilitated meetings?
- Led teams in solving problems?
- Coordinated outside vendors?
- Held a leadership position in a school organization, team, or club?
- Been elected to a post by your peers?
- Organized or coordinated significant events?
- Had a position of responsibility at a previous employer?

If you don't have a track record as a leader, you should at least be able to show accomplishments and results that will earn respect. And by all means, make sure you have some stories to tell about being a great team member.

Aspiration, Achievement, and Record of Results

More and more firms are emphasizing "results orientation" in their work with clients. Many firms now talk about both developing and implementing recommendations. The implementation is where the hard work starts, but also where the payoff is found. Firms want to know whether you have what it takes to deliver real results.

Have you

- Brought new customers and revenue into your company?
- Made something more efficient by saving money or time?
- Implemented an innovative idea?
- Improved service or responsiveness to customers?
- Set a challenging goal and achieved it?
- Solved a problem that affected your organization's ability to succeed?

If you haven't done any of these or similar things, you might want to reconsider your desire to become a consultant. These activities are part and parcel of consulting work, and your ability to perform well in a results-oriented environment will have a strong impact on your success at most firms. The need for rather specific, often quantitative, measurements of your accomplishments should start you thinking about how to track and measure your achievements if you don't already.

Industry or Functional Expertise

If you have a strong understanding of an industry and can communicate well with clients and help firms in that industry solve their problems, you may have an edge. These days clients demand consultants who are familiar with their field, can "speak the language," and can relate to their specific problems. It's a good idea to check out which firms have practice areas in your industry. They're more likely to be interested in your particular expertise.

Many firms have functional practice groups that seek people with previous work experience in areas such as supply chain management, marketing, corporate finance, human resources, customer service, and so on. If you're experienced in one of these fields, target the firms that specialize in it. You may want to check out WetFeet's Insider Guide to *Specialized Consulting Careers: Health Care, Human Resources, and Information Technology.*

Have you

- Worked in an industry for a long time?
- Held various roles within one industry?
- Been responsible for analyzing or selling to an industry?
- Held similar functional roles in different industries?
- Been able to apply your functional knowledge from one industry to another?
- Worked extensively in a specific area, such as logistics or manufacturing?
- Written a thesis or research paper about a particular industry, business issue, or other topic?
- Followed a particular industry or business topic intensively?

If not, don't despair, though you will need to be able to point to other strengths that counterbalance your lack of industry experience. This is more of a nice-to-have category in many cases, especially for undergraduates—recruiters don't expect you to have taken 3 years off to become a manufacturing guru.

Teamwork

Teamwork, with clients and other consultants, is a critical component of most, if not all, consulting assignments. Consultants constantly work in teams—project teams, joint client teams, practice development teams, sales teams, recruiting teams, and so on. The favorite consulting solution to any problem is to form a team to study it. Firms look for people who can work with others. One insider states, "We need people who can be a part of our nimble workforce" (read: forming and reforming lots of different teams). Teamwork translates to an ability to balance expressing your own opinions with listening to others and knowing when—and when not—to impose your will.

Have you

- Been a member of a sports team?
- Worked in study groups?
- Worked on political or volunteer committees?
- Planned and attended group events?

Of course you have! We don't know of any candidate, particularly one at the business school level, who hasn't been involved in working with a team (love those study groups!). Identify the teams or groups you've been a part of (there is a difference between the two—teams form around a common goal) and think about the role you typically play. If you've proven your ability to play a productive role as a team member or, better yet, to effectively lead a team, highlight it. In your interview you may be quizzed on your team involvement, the type of role you tend to play on a team, or how you've worked with a team to identify and solve a problem.

Basic Resume Don'ts and Dos

So now you know the consultants' preferred content and format and you've done some soul searching and come up with your perfect resume, right? Before you plaster it on electronic bulletin boards and send a mass mailing to every firm in *Who's Who in Consulting*, check out and avoid the mistakes commonly found in resumes and cover letters. Our insiders said the following flops were frequent offenders.

Some common consulting resume mistakes can be turned into assets. Follow these tips for building a stronger, more refined resume:

Don't use vague qualitative terms such as "large" or "many," which leave the reader with questions about specifics.

Do use numbers where appropriate to clearly describe your accomplishments, as in "led a team of nine sales reps."

Don't waste resume space with frivolous information, such as "my favorite color is blue."

Do include personal information that is relevant and gives the reader a better understanding of who you are.

Don't try to differentiate yourself with an unconventional format or tactics such as graphics and colored paper.

Do stick to a basic, clear format that helps the reader glean information quickly and with minimal effort.

Don't puff up your titles to make them sound more impressive.

Do focus on your responsibilities more than your titles, describing work performed and results achieved.

Don't try to portray yourself as a jack-of-all-trades in the hope that something will strike the reader's fancy.

Do discuss your two or three strengths and illustrate them with experience and achievement.

Don't use dramatic, self-congratulatory language to describe either your accomplishments or your suitability for consulting.

Do let your achievements speak for themselves by describing them succinctly and objectively.

Don't get caught in the passive voice trap, writing as if things happened to you.

Do use the active voice with verbs that indicate you're in charge.

Don't try to sound like an expert through the reckless use of buzzwords and industry jargon.

Do spend time on industry and company research before sending off a resume and cover letter.

Don't kiss up too obviously (as in, "I would be privileged and honored to interview with your esteemed firm, and perhaps join one of the greatest organizations in the world.")

Do take the time to mention what specifically interests you about the particular firm.

Don't even think of writing more than 1 page, unless you have more than 10 years of experience.

Do distinguish the important from the trivial in your background to fit the most relevant and significant elements onto a single page.

Buzzword Bozos and Other Big Offenders

We've talked a lot about what recruiters look for in resumes and cover letters. Well, there are also lots of things they don't like to see. If your resume fits one of these descriptions, you run a high risk of a ding, no matter how strong your qualifications are.

High Inflation Rates

Inflation rates are higher in consulting resumes than in developing countries during elections. Yeah, we know, everyone exaggerates to some extent, but insiders tell us that a resume that looks too good to be true probably is. Therefore, most of them look at a glowing resume with a heavy dose of skepticism. You need to sell yourself and showcase your talents without going overboard. The biggest mistake insiders note is the tendency to overstate experience.

The Buzzword Bozo

Buzzword bozos use words in the wrong context or words that aren't meaningful in an attempt to sound savvy. If you claim to have been "responsible for reengineering the audit approval process," you risk appearing more naive than you are. After all, "reengineering" is just another word for "changing," and "audit approval process" is redundant. Why not lose "approval" and claim to have "changed the audit process?"

The Title Titillator

Title titillators think a fancy title will make their experience sound better. Consider the very impressive-sounding title "Director of Strategic Operations." What on earth does that mean? Any consultant knows enough about how various industries are structured to be suspicious of such a title. Go with "Director of Business Development" instead. When in doubt, simplify so as to make your role and responsibilities clearer, rather than more obscure.

The Liar

Frighteningly enough, many insiders we talked to said they had caught individuals lying about everything from what degrees they had earned to where they had earned them to where they had worked. One remembered a candidate from a top finance school who had lied about being on the board of a prominent charity. It so happened that the reader's spouse was on that board, which made for a very interesting dinner table conversation that evening, and an awkward phone call to the candidate the next day. Needless to say, he was not invited for an interview.

The Novelist

Novelists typically agonize over their cover letters, thinking that their mastery of James Joyce–style prose will impress consulting recruiters. They spend countless hours tinkering with margins and font sizes to cram their life's narrative neatly onto 1 page. Offenders of this type are often using the space to explain something, such as a career change, a low GPA, or a time gap in their resume. While it's understandable to address one or two of these issues (albeit briefly) in the cover letter, it's important to keep your audience in mind. Consultants think in bullet points and key takeaways, not in densely packed prose. The longer your cover letter, the more likely the recruiter is to skim it (which effectively defeats its purpose).

Too Much of a Good Thing

Resumes that lack focus are big losers. They include mentions of membership in seven different clubs without a leadership position in any of them; experience in five industries in the past 4 years; and knowledge of marketing, sales, manufacturing, finance, and information systems. Right. Why don't such people just start their own consulting firms?

Chek You're Speling

Typos won't always get you thrown into the circular, but why take the risk? Our insiders said one typo wouldn't disqualify a candidate, but several typos probably would. On the other hand, any typo is a good enough reason to nix a candidate and, depending on the reader's mood and level of patience, a typo might be just the excuse needed to whittle down that pile. Use your spell checker, but be sure to proofread carefully. Spell checkers won't catch all typos and won't check for other hazards such as misused contractions (your vs. you're, it's vs. its, etc.). Certainly, the spell check function won't pick up mistakes in the name of the company or the recruiter (and consultants are sticklers for details like that, if you can imagine it!). If you catch a recruiter on a bad day, your references to Booz, Allen & Hamilton (when it should be Booz Allen Hamilton) might tip the scale ever-so-subtly against you. Consultants are a notoriously detail-oriented bunch, and a seemingly minor glitch might call your own attention to detail into question. Don't count on your software to make it perfect. It's always a good idea to have a friend or two read through your resume before you send it out.

Technology Hang-Ups

You may think e-mail is the best thing since the Pony Express, but that doesn't mean your recruiter does. Don't expect the person on the receiving end to fumble around with an attached file in a desperate quest to review your qualifications. If you have any doubts about the quality of the format in which your resume will arrive, because of platform or application variables, it's best to send a hard copy as well. "Nothing is worse than printing an e-mailed resume with a bunch of garbage symbols in it!" rants a recruiter. Faxing is almost as fast as e-mail, and often more reliable, although it's definitely a good idea to follow up a faxed resume with a phone call to make sure it was received in legible form.

A Note on Keywords

As you probably know, many organizations use resume-scanning software to identify qualified candidates among a sea of online applications; by scanning resumes for certain words and phrases, scanning software is intended to streamline the resume review process for time-starved recruiters, who may literally receive thousands of applications for a single job posting. As this type of software has become more prevalent, many career advisors have suggested that candidates pepper their resumes with the keywords that recruiters use most frequently to screen job applicants.

Keywords are almost always nouns or short phrases. They name the characteristics, skills, tools, training, and experience of a successful candidate for a particular job. Make sure they're included in your resume. It's likely that your resume will be entered into the firm's online database. Just as when you perform an Internet search and you view a list of hits, the resume database will scan your resume for certain keywords entered by the recruiter, who then receives a report on number of hits. The more hits, the better your chances that a recruiter will opt to read your resume.

Visit consulting firms' websites and check out the language used to describe training programs and job requirements. Even if you're applying through an on-campus recruiting process rather than responding to an online job posting, it's always a good idea to consult the job description that the company provides—as well as the list of qualifications associated with that position—to tailor and tweak the version of the resume you use to apply for that position. Meet with consultants and listen to the words they use (keeping in mind that firms specializing in a particular industry or function—such as health care or human resources, e.g.—have their own lingo as well). Here's a list (although by no means an exhaustive one) to get you started:

Industry Terms

Analysis
Applications
Applied research
Balanced scorecard
Baseline
Benchmarking
Branding
B-to-B (or B2B or business-to-business)
B-to-C (or B2C or business-to-consumer)
Business process reengineering
Case team
Change management
Commerce chain management
Consultancy
Core competencies
CRM (or customer relationship management)
E-commerce
Engagement
Enterprise application
ERP (or enterprise resource planning)
Gross margin
Internal consultant
Inventory management
Java
Just-in-time (JIT) delivery

Knowledge management

LINUX

Market segmentation

Outsourcing

Sell-through analysis

Six sigma

Supply chain

Total quality management

Personal Characteristics

Analytical ability

Attention to detail

Client focus

Communication skills

Follow-through

Intellectual curiosity

Interpersonal aptitude

Goal orientation

Motivation

Multitasking ability

Negotiating ability

Persuasiveness

Quantitative skills

Results focus

Tools

Bloomberg

Excel

Financial modeling

PowerPoint

Spreadsheet

Fair Warning

As is the case with any job search strategy, it's best to temper your enthusiasm for keywords with a healthy dose of good judgment. Particularly if you're applying for a consulting position through an on-campus recruiting process at your college or business school, your resume will be reviewed first and foremost by a human being (and quite possibly an entire committee of them who will decide on your interview fate by consensus). For better or for worse, consulting firms have their own unique set of screening criteria that enable them to pare down the consulting hopefuls from the consulting hapless, and at the resume review stage, it's typically the perceived quality of school you've attended (both undergraduate and graduate), your academic achievement (read: GPA and test scores), and the quality of your work experience to date.

As such, keep in mind that there is no magic bullet when it comes to consulting resume keywords, so don't get carried away. Never attempt to cut and splice the entire job description into the body of your resume and cover letter in an attempt to cram in as many keywords as possible. This strategy almost always backfires; to the recruiters who are reviewing your resume, you'll come across as contrived rather than credible. Recruiters live and die by the mantra "if it looks too good to be true, it probably is," so don't offend their finely tuned sensibilities by lying or exaggerating to match the job prerequisites exactly as they appear in the job posting. Rather than trying to outsmart resume scanning software, your best bet is to focus on the skills on which the consulting profession requires and writing a resume that highlights a record of sustained achievement in these areas.

Buzzword Alert!

You need to sound business-savvy, to use current terms to describe your experience and abilities. How to select from the vast array of choices, and, most important, to avoid the banal buzzwords? Use the WetFeet Resume Terms guidelines, and you will sound professional and banking-oriented without seeming desperate.

Good, Solid Terms

These words (and their variations) are specific and quantitative without being too technical, and imply worthy accomplishments.

result	measure, ~ment
yield	model
analyze	forecast
manage	conduct
lead	implement
percent, ~age	process
revenue	create

Use with Caution

These terms often tip off a reader that the writer is trying to puff, embellish, or add gloss.

consult	sophisticated
strategy/strategic	complex
liaison	successful
recommend	facilitate
work with	co-anything
assist	

Buzzword Alert! (cont'd)

These words have become practically meaningless through overuse. Or they were never real words to begin with. Either way, you can be sure that in whatever context you use them they will be "wrong" to at least one reader. Our recommendation: Avoid them.

reengineering	change management
value chain	incentivize
methodological	any *Harvard Business Review* buzzwords more than a year old

Resumes Reviewed

By this point you should have a pretty good idea of how a consulting firm handles its resumes, and you should have started thinking about how to present your own qualifications. However, the final step remains. You have to take your basic package of skills and experience and turn it into a compelling marketing piece. To illustrate many of the points we have offered so far, and to give you ideas about how to improve your presentation, we have included nine real resumes from aspiring consultants. (We've changed the names and other revealing information to protect the guilty.) We selected an assortment of people from different backgrounds, and we reviewed them as applicants for a management consulting position. We also asked our consulting insiders for comments and suggestions on how these volunteers could repackage their experience for the consulting screen. Here's what they had to say.

Resume 1: MBA with Traditional Business Background

From Being Lost in Excess . . .

See the numbered items on the resume on the following 2 pages:

1. If this info is truly important, put it in the cover letter or "Other" section.
2. This information should be omitted if you're sending your resume to a recruiter based in the United States.
3. This list is suspiciously long and should be moved to the last section.
4. This section should come after "Experience."
5. In general:

- Use the active voice.
- Show the highlights.
- Give results, not laundry-list descriptions.

6. What does this mean and why is it relevant?
7. Be specific: how big a budget?
8. Managed what size staff?
9. Raised how much capital? Turned a profit in how long?
10. Resulting in what cost reduction annually?
11. Managed how many people with what results?
12. So what?
13. Again, so what?
14. Pick one or two of these; which are most important to you?

PERSONAL DETAILS

	Name	**GRANT, Andrew Wesley**
	Address	27 Ridge View Way, Wellington, New Zealand
	Telephone	(Wk) 821 1234 5991 (Hm) 821 1234 2117 (Mobile) 0419 1234 882
1	**Nationality**	Australian and British
	Work Permits	European Union, USA, Australia, New Zealand
	Age	32
2	**Experience**	15 years work experience, including five internationally
	Family	Married with two children
3	**Interests**	Chess, Classical Guitar, Piano, Yoga, Skiing, Running, Photography, Current Affairs, Travel and the Internet

4 **EDUCATION**

MBA (Technology) – Auckland Business School, University of Auckland
(Studying part time, working full time. 15 out of 20 subjects completed. GPA:>78%)

BA (Economics) – Royal Military College, Westland University

High School Certificate – Peninsula Grammar School, Auckland

5 **EMPLOYMENT**

1996–Current **Selecta Multimedia Pty. Ltd.**

Position Marketing Manager (Full Time Consultant) 6

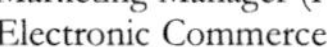

Electronic Commerce

Experience

- Complete marketing responsibility for new product development in the area of Electronic Payments via the Internet, cable, mobile, and basic telephony: market/industry research, market segmentation and sizing, focus group selection and brief, positioning, branding, pricing, and promotion. Tools used include sophisticated database and mapping techniques. Ongoing negotiation and development of channels, registration processes, and customer care
- Development and successful presentation of the Business Case and Marketing Strategy for Australian and South East Asian markets
- 7 Determination and management of budgets
- Management of cross functional team of 8
- Provision of technical / systems consultancy in areas of encryption, the Internet, business system requirements and security
- Developed object oriented model and new Internet based prototype for product conceptualisation
- Conclusion / ongoing negotiations with New Zealand financial institutions/banks, merchants and corporates, as well as (geographically dispersed) internal development team, systems integrators and suppliers

1995-Current **National Internet Pty. Ltd.**

National Internet Service Provider: Dial-up, Web Authoring, Consultancy 8

Position Founder and Managing Director

Experience

- Equity position and startup of a national Internet Service business, employing three Directors and four staff
- Providing local dial up access nationally, LAN connectivity, web authoring, data base design and business strategy (Internet) consultancy services
- Servicing consumers, small business and corporates in every mainland state
- Developed Business Plan, Technology and Marketing Strategies
- Generated profit within 18 months
- 9 Raised venture capital
- Setup national inbound/outbound telemarketing and customer care centers
- Prepared and implemented national advertising strategy (print and radio)
- Concluded negotiations for sales and service channel with partner companies in Sydney, Perth and Canberra

1992–1995 **Selecta Corporation**
New Zealand telecommunications company, $15 billion turnover; 70,000 staff

Position Senior Business Analyst (Full Time Consultant)
Corporate Systems and Processes, Corporate Finance

Experience
- Successful identification of firmwide work flow and business process redesign opportunities
- Responsible for development of Business Cases in consultation with senior management at national level for a number of applications
- Successful development and implementation of associated business requirements, functional specifications, test strategies and training in support of identified business
10 process redesign opportunities
- Prime focus on budget and forecasting Management and Executive Information Systems and processes across Selecta
- Successfully performed complex financial analysis for senior management and Selecta Board – affecting balance sheet

11 • Managed numerous teams across software development life cycle

1990–1992 **Jervis Partners Pty. Ltd.**
Commodity Traders – Precious and Non-Ferrous Metals (Family's business)

Position Manager – Commodities Trading and Risk Management

Experience
- Responsible for commodity trading in London / North American markets, and foreign exchange risk management
- Negotiated international sales purchase agreements (import and export)
- Identified new markets for buying selling of commodities globally, resulting in a 15% increase in profits
- Managed team of 5
- Managed all commodity shipments internationally
- Developed sophisticated financial and scenario modelling to tight deadlines

1989–1990 **First Boston Bank**

Position Systems Accountant
Corporate Operating Services

Experience
- Successful specification, development and implementation of Management and Executive Information Systems for European operations – within budget and on time
- Managed team of 5
- Reported to London and New York

12 **1988 to 1989** **Financial Services** – Management Accountant, **London**
Largest U.K. retail chain; 60,000 staff, £1.6 billion turnover
- Reporting to Director of Finance (Credit Cards):
- Management accounting: monthly, quarterly, year end
- Profitability, bad debt, variance, cash flow and cross spend analysis

13 **1986 to 1988** **Baden Business Publications** – Trainee Financial Accountant, **London**
German publishing company; 11,000 staff; £1.1 billion turnover, top ten worldwide
- Financial accounting: monthly, quarterly, and year end
- Monthly variance analysis and presentation to publishers and senior management
- Trial Balance
- Also worked/trained in litigation, credit control, purchase/sales ledger, payroll, and cashiers departments

1985 **National New Zealand Bank** — Undergraduate Trainee, **Auckland** (Part Time)
- Trained in Loan, Securities, Customer Service and Cashiers departments

1982 to 1984 **Westland** — Staff Cadet, Royal Military College, **Westland**
- Third youngest cadet to be accepted at Australia's most prestigious Officer Military Academy

14 **OTHER**

1996–Current Elected and actively contributing to Board of Management Synagogue
1996–1997 Elected and actively contributed to Student Council
Auckland Business School, University of Auckland
1985/86 Backpacked through North Africa, East, Central and West Europe
1981/82 Member of two month Middle East study tour (Israel, Golan, Sinai, West Bank)
1981 Completed High School Certificate at age 16
1981 Member of School Debating and Chess Teams – reached State Finals
1979–81 Attended several Outward Bound Expeditions

. . .To Focused and Relevant

Our rewrite focuses on Andrew's most recent experience and mentions only his most significant responsibilities and accomplishments. We used the active voice to create a more compelling and less narrative tone, dumped the hyperbole, and scaled way back on the additional information. The result is a resume that shows evidence of the basic consulting skills (leadership potential, analytical skills, and some level of academic achievement), highlights entrepreneurial experience and specific accomplishments, and shows experience leading teams, analyzing data, and bringing about change in an organization. Andrew now has a strong, balanced resume.

See next page.

Andrew Wesley Grant
27 Ridge View Way
Wellington, New Zealand
Telephone (Wk) 821 1234 5991 (Hm) 821 1234 2117 (Mobile) 0419 1234 882

EXPERIENCE

1996–Current **Selecta Multimedia Pty. Ltd.**
New Zealand telecommunications company, $15 billion turnover; 70,000 staff
Marketing Manager, Electronic Commerce
- Managed all marketing for new products involving electronic payments via the Internet, cable, mobile, and basic telephony. Conducted market/industry research, analyzed segments and size, and set up focus groups, positioning, branding, pricing, and promotion strategies.
- Developed business case and marketing strategy for Australian and South East Asian markets. The plan was approved and implemented, resulting in an initial market share capture of 15%.
- Managed $500,000 budget.
- Managed cross-functional team of eight.

1995–Current **National Internet Pty. Ltd.**
National Internet service company providing dial-up, Web-authoring, and consultancy services.
Founder and Managing Director
- Founded and managed national Internet service provider serving more than 5,000 consumer and business accounts.
- Developed and implemented technology and marketing strategies, negotiating contracts with partner companies.
- Raised $500,000 in venture capital and generated profit within 18 months.

1992–1995 **Selecta Corporation**
Senior Business Analyst, Corporate Systems and Processes, Corporate Finance
- Developed business cases for new IT systems proposals in consultation with senior national management.
- Identified and wrote associated business requirements, functional specifications, test strategies and training programs in support of business process redesign opportunities resulting in a cost reduction of $50,000 annually.
- Performed complex financial analysis for senior management and Selecta Board, which resulted in changes to the balance sheet.
- Managed three teams across software development life cycle to deliver projects on time and on budget.

1990–1992 **Jervis Partners Pty. Ltd.**
Commodity Traders – Precious and Non-Ferrous Metals
Manager – Commodities Trading and Risk Management
- Identified new markets for buying and selling of commodities globally, resulting in a 15% increase in profits.
- Managed team of five.

EDUCATION

MBA (Technology) – Auckland Business School, University of Auckland
(Studying part-time, working full-time. 15 out of 20 subjects completed.)

BA (Economics) – Royal Military College, Westland University 1985

OTHER

Member of synagogue board of management.
Elected to Student Council, Auckland Business School, University of Auckland.
Interested in chess, classical guitar, current affairs, and the Internet.

Resume 2: MBA with Traditional Business Background

From Weak Results . . .

This list references the numbered items on the next page:

1. Who? How big?
2. What's your role?
3. What's the result?
4. Conducted? Attended?
5. To do what?
6. What was your role? What was the outcome?
7. Second-tier school—need to see some academic strength here.
8. How selected?
9. Big or small? How many students?
10. Top percent of class?

"Gerald's background probably has many of the elements we'd look for, but I don't get the feeling he'd be a good consultant because there is no indication that he's strived for measured results in his professional endeavors," one reviewer tells us. Another cautions, "Without a degree at a top school, he'd need outstanding experience to pass the screen at our firm, and this candidate just doesn't have it. He might be suitable for one of our European offices." The truth isn't always pretty, but you need someone to give you the straight scoop!

The format of Gerald's resume is excellent: dates on the left, logical sequencing, companies and titles clearly indicated, and concise bullets. But the sentence structure for the bullets should be parallel—each sentence should start with an active verb. In addition, there's no evidence of academic achievement.

GERALD MAILLAND

306 Green Road
Rochester, NY 27410

Tel. (Home): 901 555 1821
Tel. (Work): 901 555 3000
Email: gerald@ccm.com

Experience

Aug. 1996 to date — **OMNI SURGICAL, S.A.** — **ROCHESTER, NY**
Research Analyst – New Markets

- Mexico and Central America
  Given the task to develop a market penetration strategy and its implementation. 
  Establishing an office in Mexico. Selection of potential distributors.
- Medical Device Product Manager
  Identified a new market and assessed its possibilities.
  Presented the project to the CEO and the Holding Company Director. 
  Led the product development team and carried out its market entry with the Regional Sales Manager.
- Training at European offices in France and the Netherlands.

Jan.–June 1995 — **J. WALTER THOMPSON LATIN AMERICA** — **MEXICO D.F., MEXICO**
Marketing Analyst – GENERAL MILLS account

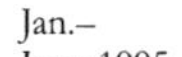

- Analysis of General Mills's allocation of advertising resources throughout Latin America.
- Created a P&L program and a database for the eight Latin American subsidiaries.
- Proposal on chocolate Ready to Eat Cereal's segment.
- Research on media analysis and planning.
- Presentations to General Mills's executives after internal review with the account Vice President.

Summer 1994 — **OMNI SURGICAL, S.A.** — **PARIS, FRANCE**
Intern – Controller's department

- Assisted in the development of a valuation tool for contracts.
- Developed a valuation approach for export contracts.
- Corrected the control method of export margins.
- Executed a valuation of total sales & rentals and related analysis.

Summer 1993 — **ELECTRICITE DE FRANCE** — **BORDEAUX, FRANCE**
Intern – Controller's department

- Forecast analysis of the electric utility market in South West France.
- Updated the "Report on External and Internal Diagnosis of the Company."

Education

1994-1995 — **GEORGE MASON UNIVERSITY**  — **WASHINGTON, D.C.**
Master of Business Administration, Class of 1996.
Concentration in Global Marketing and Entrepreneurship.
One out of the two first students jointly sponsored by ESLSCA and GMU to attend Graduate School.

1992–1994 — **NOTRE DAME BUSINESS SCHOOL** — **PARIS, FRANCE**
Business degree, December 1995, International Business.
Ski team captain, co-creator of the baseball team. A.I.E.S.E.C. member.
Organizer of "International Week" welcoming East European business students. 

1991–1992 — **LEROI PREPARATORY BUSINESS SCHOOL** — **BORDEAUX, FRANCE**
Co-creator and editor of the school's newspaper.

1990–1991 — **EXCHANGE STUDENT, REDMOND SENIOR HIGH SCHOOL** — **MINNEAPOLIS, MN**
Graduated class of 1991. Academic Achievement Award.

Language Skills — Fluent French and English, proficient Spanish, started Japanese.
Computer — IBM compatible systems, Microsoft Office, Netscape. Programming in Turbo Pascal.
Personal — Special interest in Latin America and Asia. Backpacked through Central and South America.

. . . To Specific Strengths

Our rewrite requires that Gerald put some thought into how to quantify his accomplishments. This does not have to entail numbers, but he must show that he's tracking his performance somehow. His strengths include a solid international background, good research and analytical skills, marketing knowledge, and lots of experience developing proposals, which comes in handy in consulting during business development pushes. He needs to showcase these strengths if he wants a chance at an interview. The resume on the next page is a great example of how to do this.

In addition to improving his resume with quantitative results, Gerald will probably need to take other steps to successfully secure an interview for a consulting position. To start, he should contact alums from his business school, set up informational interviews with them, and really seek to understand the industry and the players. He may want to target some boutique firms that would value his language skills and international experience. One possibility would be to consider firms that focus on providing advice about Latin America. Alternatively, Gerald might have better luck approaching firms with an interest in Latin American markets, especially in the consumer goods industry. Finally, because his resume doesn't jump out of the stack, Gerald will want to really have his story down cold about why he wants to work for a particular company and what he can bring to it that is unique.

GERALD MAILLAND
306 Green Road Tel. (Home): 901 555 1821
Rochester, NY 27410 Tel. (Work): 901 555 3000
Email: gerald@ccm.com

Experience

Aug. 1996 to date

OMNI SURGICAL , S.A. — **Rochester, NY**
(Surgical equipment manufacturer—$55 million, sales)
Research Analyst — New Markets
- Conducted a detailed study of the medical device market in Mexico. Managed a two-month research effort, including surveys, interviews and customer visits.
- Identified a new $10 million market, and drafted and presented a market penetration strategy to CEO.
- Led five-person product development team and implemented market entry strategy with Regional Sales Manager.
- Established a new three-person office in Mexico City.
- Identified eight potential distributors and negotiated distribution agreements.

Jan. to June 1995

J. WALTER THOMPSON LATIN AMERICA — **Mexico D.F., Mexico**
Marketing Analyst — GENERAL MILLS account
- Analyzed effectiveness of General Mills's $25 million Latin America advertising budget, and proposed reallocation of one-third of budget to higher value channels.
- Created the first standard P&L worksheet covering eight Latin American subsidiaries, which improved cash forecasting capabilities, and allowed office-by-office profit analysis.
- Proposed a brand extension strategy for the chocolate Ready to Eat cereal market, which formed the basis of new product development efforts.
- Made regular presentations about business unit performance to executive committee.

Summer 1994

OMNI SURGICAL, S.A. — **Paris, France**
Intern — Controller's Department
- Devised a valuation tool to analyze lifetime cost of manufacturing equipment contracts and maintenance.
- Developed a valuation system for export contracts that captured exchange rate fluctuations.
- Improved the system for estimating and setting export contract profit hurdles.

Summer 1993

ELECTRICITE DE FRANCE — **Bordeaux, France**
Intern — Controller's Department
- Forecasted electricity demand in Southwest France as a basis for bringing on additional generating capacity.
- Researched company's internal structure and external market position, and revised the standard company operating procedures manual used by 75,000 employees.

Education

1994–1995

GEORGE MASON UNIVERSITY — **Washington, D.C.**
Master of Business Administration, Class of 1996
Concentrating on Global Marketing and Entrepreneurship.
One of only two students to qualify, based on 3.8 GPA in first term, for Graduate School sponsorship from ESLSCA and GMU.

1992–1994

NOTRE DAME BUSINESS SCHOOL — **Paris, France**
Bachelor of Business, December 1995, International Business.
Ski team captain, co-creator of the baseball team. A.I.E.S.E.C. member.
Organized "International Week" welcoming Eastern European students.

1991–1992

LEROI PREPARATORY BUSINESS SCHOOL — **Bordeaux, France**
Co-creator and editor of the school newspaper.

1990–1991

EXCHANGE STUDENT, REDMOND SR. H.S. — **Minneapolis, MN**
Graduated in top 5% of class and won Academic Achievement Award.

Other

Fluent in French and English, proficient in Spanish, starting Japanese.

Resume 3: MBA with Small Company Experience

A Model of Excellence

"Robert's resume is a very easy read. Even at first glance he looks like a strong candidate. We like to see a high GPA like his, especially when he's from a less well-known school. And the fact that he's achieved a lot in both entrepreneurial and corporate settings indicates that he'd do well at our firm and with a variety of clients."

Even though most of Robert's experience is at a small, unknown company, the explanation of his role, work performed, results achieved, and career progression is so clear and thoughtful that the company becomes almost irrelevant. Would it be stronger if his experience were at Intel? Maybe, but then we'd wonder why he went to business school at all. . . .

He has clearly described his role and neatly summarized his responsibilities at the top of each section. The points in the bullets illustrate specific, quantified results achieved through research, analysis, and modeling. In addition, Robert gives examples of team involvement, management experience, and leadership potential through his summer employment and activities.

In spite of all of these strengths, we have a few suggestions to enhance Robert's resume:

1. He should lead with his experience, since that is his strength.
2. Move the dates to the left margin under experience so that they don't become lost in the locations.
3. Add a location for the GE experience.

ROBERT A. MacPHERSON
422 Applegate Blvd., #633
Pittsburgh, PA 15102
(412) 555-5566
E-mail: bob@macpherson.com

EDUCATION: **CARNEGIE MELLON UNIVERSITY** **Pittsburgh, PA**
Candidate for MBA Degree to be awarded June 1998
GPA: 3.92

BATES COLLEGE **Lewiston, ME**
B.A., History, June 1990
National Merit Scholar

EXPERIENCE: **MARKETING ASSOCIATE** **November 1996–present** 2
GE – Health Care Division

Work directly with technical and marketing professionals in the design and strategic positioning of high-tech surgical products.

- Co-leader of project team that is developing a surgical product to be used in image-guided neuro-surgery. My role is to perform strategic market analysis, work directly with end-users to identify key product attributes, and implement global product roll-out.
- Work directly with global product manager and European and Asian marketing managers as lead analyst on long-term, world-wide product strategy. Responsible for identifying global competitive threats and opportunities, evaluating regional and local market trends, and making recommendations for systematic market penetration.

GENERAL MANAGER **October 1993–July 1996**
Delivery Express **St. Louis, Missouri**
Developed strategic systems and managed day-to-day operations for $1.1 million same-day delivery firm.

- Instituted changes within the firm which directly led to sales growth from $250,000 to over $1 million in lessthan three years.
- Performed market price analysis and customer price elasticity study to determine optimal service pricing and employee compensation levels. Persuaded company president to make changes to these systems that generated 10% increase in net revenue and 80% increase in net profit.
- Created logistical model for customer-specific delivery systems that was initially applied to two accounts that totaled 5% of net income. The increased efficiency from this model delivered a 30% increase in net profit while generating 66% improvement in customers' ability to meet critical time parameters. Model was subsequently applied to all accounts in scheduled delivery division.
- Worked directly with client team from a chemical supply firm to customize distribution system. This required careful process mapping, rationalization of service options, and creation of a pull-through vendor-managed delivery system.
  This system eliminated product delivery delays and reduced order cycle times to less than 24 hours while reducing the customers' costs by over 15%.
- Used multiple regression analysis to model optimal staff levels and strategically target recruiting efforts. Process rationalization reduced contractor turnover by 50% and recruiting costs by over 70%.

MANAGER, BICYCLE DIVISION **September 1991– October 1993**
Delivery Express **St. Louis, Missouri**
Directed day-to-day operations of twenty bicycle messengers and two dispatchers.

- Instituted performance standard measurement tools that defined expectations for back-office staff based on analytical performance measures.
- Used competitive benchmarking to establish quantitative goals for critical service parameters. Achieved unprecedented 99.6% on-time delivery rate for bicycle division.

ACTIVITIES AND HONORS:
President, CMU MBA Association (May 1997 – May 1998)
Co-Founder and Chair, CMU Consulting Club (September 1996)
Team Leader, CMU Volunteer Consulting Project (September 1996 – January 1997)
Finalist, "Most Valuable Student Award" – Nominated by peers (May 1997)

Resume 4: MBA with Nontraditional Business Background

From Prolific Prose . . .

This list references the numbered items on the next page:

1. Lose this. Doesn't add value.
2. Second-tier school; don't focus here first.
3. This will barely make it.
4. What is this? Was he working while going to school?
5. Not good enough to include.
6. Good! Uses active voice and gives results.
7. Bullets, please! Does he expect me to read this entire paragraph word-for-word?
8. Too much info, most of it unhelpful.
9. Nice, but you're not going to be touring Spain during client travel assignments.
10. Why total? As opposed to 4 years not totaled?
11. Yes, we assume this if you're interested in consulting. Consultants do travel.

MICHAEL D. NEWMAN

987 Cantilever Court
Weston, MA 02123
(508) 555-9021

1 **CAREER SUMMARY**

Engineering services and management generalist with over 7 years of experience in a diversified industry. Seeking position as management consultant with emphasis on operations and decision support.

EDUCATION

BABSON COLLEGE 2 **Wellesley, MA**
Graduate School of Business Administration **GPA 3.7/4.0** 3
Candidate for Master of Business Administration, May 1998
4 Charter Member, Part-Time MBA Association

OLD DOMINION UNIVERSITY **Norfolk, VA**
Bachelor of Science, Mechanical Engineering **GPA 3.0/4.0** 5

EXPERIENCE 1990 – 1997

NAVAL SHIPYARD **New London, CT**
Project Engineer
6 Coordinated contracts and services of seven engineering divisions for over twenty-seven projects valued at $25.9 million. Compiled, presented, and
7 defended manning and budget proposals for all assigned projects. Led a successful process improvement initiative to double the quality of cost estimates and managed implementation of team recommendations. Oversaw development and maintenance of twenty-three process instructions used to ensure the quality and consistency of engineering services, including process instructions for planning, estimating, and engineering nuclear projects. Developed and maintained a database of manning and budget data for a department of over 400 engineers and technical professionals and utilized this resource to develop departmental budget and staffing plans. Received Outstanding Achievement Award for development and presentation of five-year personnel hiring plan. Initiated and participated in development of departmental technical resources management system estimated to reduce engineering cost by $52,000 per year. Developed policy for and maintained functional control over departmental intranet. Developed process for and maintained functional control over electronic distribution system for all nuclear process instructions.

Lead Instructor, Nuclear Training
Developed, coordinated and conducted training program for engineering personnel responsible for directing nuclear reactor systems testing for submarines. Oversaw preparation and administration of qualification examinations for a division of over 100 personnel.

Testing Support, Nuclear Engineering
Wrote technical procedures for and assisted in oversight of on-site post-repair testing of reactor plant systems.

8 **PERSONAL**

Skilled in WORD, EXCEL, MINITAB, WORDPERFECT, and POWERPOINT. Skilled in use of decision support programs LINDO and DATA. Working knowledge of PROJECT, VISIO, and FOXPRO. Read/write Spanish,
9 10 communicate verbally at tourist level. Four years total experience as editor of Mace & Crown and County Dance News. Willing to relocate/travel. 11

. . .To Targeted Bullets

Here's our rewrite of Michael's most recent experience, with bullets, of course:

EXPERIENCE **NAVAL SHIPYARD** **New London, CT**
1990–1997 **Project Engineer**

Responsible for coordinating contracts, budgets, and services of seven engineering divisions for 27 projects valued at $25.9 million.

- Led a process improvement initiative that doubled the quality of cost estimates, resulting in $2 million annual cost reductions.
- Created departmental staffing and budget plans by developing and maintaining a database of manning and budget information for a department of more than 400 professionals.
- Earned Outstanding Achievement Award for development and presentation of five-year personnel hiring plan.
- Initiated technical resources management system estimated to reduce engineering costs by 12% per year.
- Developed policy for and maintained functional control over departmental intranet serving 130 users.

Michael should add a summary of responsibilities, as we've done, making sure that it's short but captures the essence of his role as project engineer. Note that in describing his accomplishments we omitted some of the fluff words, such as "successful," and added information on specific results achieved, to clarify Michael's depth of responsibility. We exchanged the dollar figure for a percent, because 12 percent is more impressive than $52,000, which is the loaded equivalent of less than one engineer.

Resume 5: PhD with Non-Business Background

From Take My Word for It . . .

This list references the numbered items on the facing page:

1. How significant are these? How much money?
2. Indicate skills by showing experience.
3. Good, but how would this be relevant to consulting?
4. Sort of a jumble—need to illustrate with better examples.
5. No clear evidence of achievement, not to mention a very unfortunate typo on the second line.
6. What? This makes me worry that he'd wax scientific and lose sight of the business fundamentals.

2–6. Combine these sections, make chronological, illustrate work performed and achieved.

Overall: Does this guy have enough business knowledge to have an impact on clients? Readers would be skeptical. . . .

BRANDON R. SHEA

OFFICE:

Physics Department
Massachusetts Institute of Technology
Cambridge, MA, 02134
617 555 7854

HOME:

245 S. Braithwaite Ave. # 201
Boston, MA 02140
617 555 1244

EDUCATION

Ph.D., Physics — Sept. 1991
Harvard University, Cambridge, MA

B.A., Physics (with highest honors) — May 1986
Oberlin College, Oberlin, OH

1 FELLOWSHIPS AND AWARDS

1995	United States National Science Foundation, International Fellow (Japan)
1995	Japan Society for the Promotion of Science, Invitation Fellow
1993	Alton Bergmann Research Publication Award
1991	Achievement Research for College Scientists Fellow

2 TECHNICAL SKILLS

Analysis of complex data. Numerical modeling. Code development on parallel supercomputers. Extraction of signals from noise. Image processing. Technical and proposal writing. Undergraduate instruction (see teaching experience, below).

3 MANAGERIAL AND TEAM EXPERIENCE

4 Supervised MIT Monitor Pulsar Project. Coordinated multi-institute NASA observing proposals. Served as principal investigator and coinvestigator on successful U.S., European, and Japanese observing programs. Frequent visits to Japan and Europe for collaborative research and preparation of scientific papers. Supervised graduate and undergraduate students.

5 RESEARCH EXPERIENCE AND ACHIEVEMENTS

SENIOR RESEARCH FELLOW, MIT	1994 to present
RESEARCH ASS OCIATE, University of Utrecht, The Netherlands	1991-1994
RESEARCH ASSISTANT, Harvard University and Institute of Space and Astronautical Science, Frankfurt, Germany	1988-1991

6 Developed computationally efficient technique for signal detection with parallel supercomputers. Compiled major review paper on accreting pulsars. Discovered microsecond time lags in a new coronal diagnostic in binary stars. Developed optimal techniques for measuring time differences between noisy aperiodic signals. Helped develop data acquisition and refrigeration systems of the Harvard neutrino detector. Initiated and helped coordinate two world-wide astronomical observing campaigns.

TEACHING EXPERIENCE

1996–1997	Mentor, Summer Undergraduate Research Fellowship Program, MIT
1997	Summer Instructor, Physics Department, Rice University
1991	Supervisor and Instructor, Oberlin College Winter Term Project
1986–1987	Teaching Assistant, Physics Department, Harvard University
1984–1986	Tutor, Physics and Mathematics Departments, Oberlin College

PERSONAL

Engineering Management Certificate, MIT Industrial Relations Office
Languages: Japanese, Dutch, and German

. . . To Some Bona Fide Experience

"Brandon's experience just doesn't seem relevant to consulting," notes one of our reviewers. "I question his ability to add value in a business situation." This one is a real stretch, but we think there's hope for Brandon. After all, someone with a PhD in physics has to be smart, right? (Big point for intellectual capacity!) Brandon's challenge is to beef up the information in the other checklist areas: leadership, record of results, and analytical skills.

Brandon's uncommon background, coupled with a nonstandard resume format, may confuse readers who are used to looking for top schools and GPAs. Brandon should definitely put his resume into the standard three-section format to help reviewers sift through his credentials.

We suggest the formatting on the following page:

BRANDON R. SHEA
245 S. Braithwaite Ave. #201, Boston, MA 02140
Home: (617) 555–1244 Office: (617) 555–7854
brandon_shea@mit.edu

Experience

1994 to current **Senior Research Fellow** Massachusetts Institute of Technology, Cambridge, MA
- Supervised Monitor pulsar project. Managed staff of four analysts.
- Responsible for structuring standard analysis, monitoring campaign, and publishing findings.
- Analyzed very large quantity of data drawn from many sources with significant variability. Developed analysis techniques and numerical models to illustrate project findings.

1997 **Summer Instructor** University of Southern California, Los Angeles, CA
- Developed the curriculum for a three-month class in only one week, cutting the standard development time by 70%.
- Received the highest ratings from student reviews ever received for a scientific class.

1996 **Member, Board of Directors** Colton Homeowner's Association, Pasadena, CA
- Elected to Board of Directors of 100-member homeowner's organization.
- Responsible for managing $150,000 budget and negotiating contracts.
- Identified opportunity for management improvements that resulted in 20% annual savings in homeowners' costs.

1991–1994 **Research Associate** University of Utrecht, The Netherlands
- Developed a computationally efficient technique for signal detection with parallel supercomputers.
- Discovered microsecond time lags in binary stars, and developed optimal techniques for measuring time differences between noisy aperiodic signals.

1988–1991 **Research Assistant** Harvard University, Cambridge, MA
- Promoted from Teaching Assistant.
- Initiated worldwide campaign to observe an astronomical object.
- Published four papers that helped solve a long-standing problem related to binary stars.
- Became the youngest recipient of the Alton Bergmann Research Publication Award for excellence in scientific publishing.

Education

MASSACHUSETTS INSTITUTE OF TECHNOLOGY Cambridge, MA
Engineering Management Certificate, 1997.
Coursework included general business and management topics.

HARVARD UNIVERSITY Cambridge, MA
Ph.D., Physics, September 1991.

OBERLIN COLLEGE Oberlin, OH
B.A., Physics, with Highest Honors, May 1986.

Other Fluent in Dutch, Japanese, and German.
Active swimmer and member of the Harvard cycling team.

Resume 6: Basic Undergraduate

From Light on Details . . .

Note: This resume would be a ding or borderline at most firms—the high grades might entice a reviewer, but high grades aren't enough. . . .

This list references the numbered items on the facing page:

1. Probably not relevant to consulting, so why add?
2. Good GPA—makes the mark.

3–4. What kind of companies are KidSoft and Webstreet? How big are they?

5. Good.
6. How much money managed?
7. Note in "Education" section.
8. Not necessary.
9. Funny, but off-beat; would go over well in some places, may not at others.

NATHAN ROSENBERG
3446 30th Street
San Francisco, CA 94114
(415) 555-2429
nathan@earthlink.com

EDUCATION:

Dartmouth College, Hanover, NH
Bachelor of Arts in English, 12/95
–Substantial additional course work in global environmental issues ❶
–GPA: 3.8 ❷

EXPERIENCE:

❸ Kidsoft, San Mateo, CA
Technical Writer, 10/96-present
–Wrote text for children's software

❹ Webstreet, San Francisco, CA
Copywriter/Database Editor, 7/96–8/96
–Wrote ad copy for the World Wide Web
– Edited FileMaker Pro database

New Hampshire Conference Center, Hanover, NH
Dining Room Floor Manager, 4/96–6/96
–Supervised staff of 15 servers and bussers ❺
–Managed deluxe meal service to 150 guests ❻
Summer Staffer, 6/94–9/94, 6/95–9/95
–Developed and implemented programs for kids' groups

Chacra Millalen, El Hoyo, Argentina
Farm Hand, 1/96–2/96
–Tended large, organic, biointensive garden
–Prepared meals for 10–20 people

The Weekly Review, Amos Tuck Graduate School of Business, Hanover, N.H.
Layout Manager, 9/95-12/95
–Duties included copy editing and layout of a bi-weekly newspaper

ADDITIONAL INFORMATION:
–Published article in Winter '95 issue of SOMA magazine
–Member, Phi Beta Kappa ❼
–Fluent in Spanish
❽ –Familiar with Macintosh and Windows (proficient on software such as Word, Excel, Photoshop, and FileMaker Pro)
–Extensive volunteer experience with at-risk youth
–Can play guitar and harmonica simultaneously ❾

. . . To Convincing

Here is our recommendation for a rewrite of portions of Nathan's experience. Through conversations with him we uncovered additional relevant tasks that he had performed while employed at each of these companies, but that he hadn't believed were important for his resume:

10/96–present

Kidsoft, Inc., a $14 million software company

Technical Writer

- Wrote text for educational software targeting children.
- Evaluated competitive products and created new format for best-of-class documentation in children's educational game market.
- Was named "most valuable team member" by peers for work in communication and coordination across products.

7/96–8/96

Webstreet, an online e-mail startup

Copywriter/Database Editor

- Created and maintained database to manage a dynamic portfolio of product text.
- Responsible for writing, reviewing and editing text for more than 30 greeting products.
- Developed several innovative greeting concepts that became profitable new product lines.

Resume 7: Undergraduate with Volunteer Experience

From Very Good . . .

This list references the numbered items on the next page:

1. Need e-mail address!
2. Excellent academic—top schools and grades.
3. What has she done related to this? Clubs? Coursework?
4. Use "Experience" instead of "Honors and Activities."
5. Bullet each of these positions.
6. Move dates to left margin.
7. Many school activities—shows balance, leadership, and initiative.
8. Many honors—sounds good, but is it real?
9. Delete this.
10. What kind of work?
11. TYPO!! NO-NO!!
12. Not helpful; better to show evidence of these skills through experience.
13. You want to be a typist?
14. Not needed.

Amy Y. Chan

1

Summer address:
1642 Oxford Terrace
Palo Alto, CA 94305
(415) 555-5969

Home address:
1465 Kapiolani Blvd, #2222
Honolulu, HI 96817
(808) 555-7854

2 *EDUCATION:*

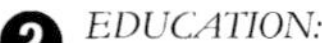

Princeton University, Princeton, NJ. Anticipated BA degree, June 1999. Senior status. GPA: 3.9/4.0. Double Major: International Relations and American Studies. Strong interest in Business/Management and Public Policy. 3

Punahou High School, Honolulu, HI. Graduated May 1995. Valedictorian. GPA: 4.0/4.0. National Merit Scholar. Earned college credit in English, Calculus, Physics, Spanish.

University of Hawaii, Honolulu, HI, Summer 1991 and 1993. GPA: 4.0/4.0. Coursework included Spanish, Honors English Literature and Exposition.

HONORS AND ACTIVITIES:

4

5 **University Undergraduate Student Government**, elected Secretary of Class of 1999. Initiated activities to promote class spirit and unity among 1200 undergraduates. Headed publicity committee and facilitated communication with students.

President of Volunteer Organization, 1994-95 school year. 6
Coordinated frequent volunteer projects with over 35 community organizations.
Presided at weekly meetings with over 60 students to discuss volunteer opportunities.
Honored at Samantha Stone international competition for Service to Community.
Honored in 15th Annual Volunteer Service Awards of Honolulu.

Commissioner of Community Action, Student Government Executive Board, 94–95.
Acting liaison between school and community for all school-wide projects.
Head Coordinator of canned food drives, clothing drives, Volunteer Week (school-wide event to promote healthy, drug-free alternatives to substance abuse).

Vice-President (2 Years), Spanish Club, 1993–94 and 1994–95 school years.
Started organization at school. Planned activities to promote language and cultural exploration. 7
First Place honors at State Declamation Foreign Language Championships. 8

9 *WORK EXPERIENCE:*

Public Relations Intern, Smith Communications, San Francisco, CA. Summer 1997.
10 Currently working with Senior Account Executives on managing clients specializing in emerging high technology and healthcare areas.

Director of Youth Program, Volunteer Center of San Diego. San Diego, CA. 6/96–9/96. Led the start-up and development of a youth volunteer program connecting 50 high schools with community organizations. Entailed extensive research. Created database of surrounding schools.

Library staff, West Street Library, Wellesley, MA. 9/95–5/96.
Managed front desk and circulation records.

Peer tutor, Honolulu, HI. 1993–94 and 1994–95 school years.
Provided private assistance for high school students.

11 *SMMARY OF SKILLS:*

–Extensive experience as Projects Coordinator, with excellent communications skills. 12
–Proficient with MS Word, Excel, WordPerfect, Netscape. Typing speed 80 wpm. 13
–High degree of competency in written and spoken Spanish.
–Quick-learning worker with analytical skills and proven leadership capabilities.

14 References readily available upon request.

. . . To Nearly Perfect

While Amy's resume is very good, we have a few questions and suggestions. For her experience section, she should select the most important activities and experience and list them chronologically. We recommend reverse chronological order. She also needs to describe the work she performed as a PR intern. Did she do research, write reports, resolve client issues? The inclusion of her work as director of a youth program is good, but what type of research was conducted? Market research? Competitive research? What kind of database was created and for what purpose? The mention of her experience as a library staff member looks strange because it occurred during the school year in Wellesley, MA, during what would have been her first year at Princeton. We immediately wonder whether she started out at Princeton, or whether she completed her first year of college at another university. This probably wouldn't affect the decision to offer an interview, but it is a distraction that would definitely be addressed early in an interview. The rest of the information in the "Work Experience" section can be included elsewhere in the resume or is superfluous. She should move the Student Government mention to the "Education" section. And if she feels it's important, she can mention the Foreign Language First Place in the "Other" section, where she talks about her Spanish language competency.

The summary of skills section is not necessary for a consulting resume because firms already know what they're looking for. Including information on standard software packages is unnecessary. Including typing speed is unnecessary unless you're looking for a position as an assistant rather than a consultant. Amy says she's a quick study, and we'll take her word for it because of her grades. But she also claims to have analytical skills, although there is no evidence in the resume of how or when they've been used.

We suggest the rewrite on the following page.

Amy Y. Chan

amy_chan@URL.com
Present address: 1642 Oxford Terrace, Palo Alto, CA 94305; (415) 555-5969
Home address: 1465 Kapiolani Blvd., #2222, Honolulu, HI 96817; (808) 555-7854

Education

Princeton University **Princeton, NJ**
GPA: 3.9

- B.A. expected June 1999. Double major in International Relations and American Studies. Extensive coursework (approximately 15 credits each) in Business/Management and Public Policy departments.
- Secretary of Class of 1999. Elected by peers to plan activities that promote class spirit and unity among 1200 undergraduates. Head publicity committee to promote major class events.

Punahou High School **Honolulu, HI**
GPA: 4.0

Graduated May 1995. Class valedictorian. National Merit Scholar. Earned college credit in English, Calculus, Physics, and Spanish.

Work Experience

Smith Communications **San Francisco, CA**
Public Relations Intern
Summer 1997 to present

- Work with senior account executives to manage relationships with clients in emerging high technology and healthcare industries.
- Assist with the writing, editing, production, and distribution of press materials, including press releases and fact sheets.
- Conduct account-related research and compiled findings into complete coverage reports.
- Develop and maintain media lists and editorial calendars.
- Collaborate with office staff to devise publicity strategy and coordinate publicity logistics for major client events.

Volunteer Center of San Diego **San Diego, CA**
Director of Youth Programs
Summer of 1996

- Led the start-up and development of a youth volunteer program that connects 50 high schools with community organizations in need of volunteers.
- Conducted extensive research to identify participating community organizations, interview organizations' leadership, and determine their most immediate volunteer needs.
- Created a comprehensive database of area schools that enabled program to effectively match student volunteers and community groups.

West Street Library **Wellesley, MA**
Library Staff
September 1995 to May 1996

- Managed front desk and circulation records.
- Worked part time while completing first year of college in Wellesley, MA: worked an average of 10–15 hours per week while maintaining a full course load.

Personal

- High degree of competency in written and spoken Spanish (founded high school Spanish club; received first place honors at State Declamation Foreign Language Championships, 1995).
- Demonstrated interest in community service initiatives (president of high school volunteer organization; honored at 15th Annual Volunteer Awards of Honolulu).

Resume 8: Undergraduate with Scientific Background

From Unfocused on Consulting . . .

This list references the numbered items on the next page:

1. Relevant? Depends on desired type of consulting.

2. Bullets would make this easier to read.

3. Not clear how significant these research projects are.

4. Analytical? Theoretical? What types of techniques?

5. Is this a team experience?

6. Move together—delete a space.

7. Good—tells us she's not just science-oriented, has a sense of humor; shows critical balance.

8. Funny!

Christine's resume indicates decent academic achievement in a competitive major usually frequented by pre-meds. Her standardized test scores show that she's not just a science geek. Her experience is very science-focused so she will need to clarify her roles in terms that are appealing to consultants. In all fairness, however, undergraduates are not expected to have nearly the business experience or acumen expected of MBAs and experienced hires.

Christine Elaine DeMichele
cdemichele@fas.harvard.edu

Present Address
Mather House #421
Cambridge, MA 02138
(617) 555–5596

Permanent Address
1263 33rd Ave.
San Francisco, CA 94123
(415) 555–1258

EDUCATION

Harvard University, Cambridge, Massachusetts.
Candidate for B.S. in Biological Sciences, June 1997
–Overall GPA 3.74/4.0 SAT Math 740 Verbal 710
1 –Presidential Scholar (one of 68 for the Class of 1997).
–Selected coursework includes: computer programming, computer consulting, and statistics.

Rockridge High School, San Francisco, California.
Graduated in June 1993.

---

2 EXPERIENCE

Department of Biological Sciences, Harvard College. *1/97–present, 1/96–6/96*
Biology 201 and 202 Senior Course Assistant: Supervise a weekly 5-hour core experimental laboratory course on plant physiology and animal behavior, respectively. Deliver weekly 45-minute lecture/slide show, help students design and run experiments, and teach students statistics and analysis of observed data sets. Also, serve as mentor and advisor to select group of students. (This course is required for all biology majors at Harvard College.)

Department of Dermatology, Harvard Medical Center. *4/96–9/96*
3 Undergraduate Researcher: Worked on an independent project involving the production and characterization of polyclonal antibodies. Utilized molecular biology techniques. 4
Brainstormed various methods to bypass problems with past experimental protocols.

Massachusetts General Hospital Diabetes Center, Boston, MA. *6/95–9/95*
Researcher: Studied complications of diabetes mellitus at Mass General, concentrating on the eye. My project involved studying the effects of glucose concentration on pericyte growth. Assisted other lab members in carrying out experiments. 5

Exxon Chemical Company, Houston, Texas. *6/94–9/94*
Process Technician: Conducted bench-scale polymerization runs and polyester recycling studies. Data entry and analysis.

6

6/93–9/93
Analytical Laboratory Assistant: Conducted polymer characterization tests. Assisted with implementation of new test procedures. Data entry.

---

7 RELATED ACTIVITIES

Computer Lab, Harvard College *Spring 1996*
Computer Consultant Intern: Assisted members of the Harvard community with computer-related problems in a Macintosh-based computer cluster.

The Harvard Crimson, Harvard College. *1/95–2/96*
Columnist: Co-created and co-wrote "The Daily Grind," a satirical column that depicted the lives
8 of five college students as they searched for good grades, romance, and some sort of explanation for why they were getting neither.

Harvard Hotline, Harvard College *1993–1994*
Peer Counselor: Fielded phone calls from members of the Harvard community who were upset, depressed, or just needed someone to talk to.

. . . To Consulting-Friendly

In the two rewritten examples on the next page, we've tried to explain what Christine has done in terms relevant to consulting. We've used bullets, of course, to enable the reader to zero in on some of her achievements. And we've sprinkled in some of our preferred terms in places where appropriate to the work she's done.

The activities mentioned in the "Related Activities" section provide a critical balance to our view of Christine as a very scientific, analytical person. We might wonder about her ability to operate in a team environment, to work with people, and to think creatively. With the addition of her experience as a columnist, which is very cleverly described, as well as her role as a peer counselor, we can assume that she has at least the minimum necessary people skills.

Christine Elaine DeMichele

cdemichele@fas.harvard.edu

Present address
Mather House #421
Cambridge, MA 02138
(617) 555-5596

Home address
1263 33rd Avenue
San Francisco, CA 94123
(415) 555-1258

Education

Harvard University — **Cambridge, MA**

- Candidate for B.S. in Biological Sciences, June 1997. Extensive coursework in computer programming, computer consulting, and statistics. — GPA: 3.74
- Named a Presidential Scholar (one of 68) for class of 1997. Selection based on academic achievement, leadership, and service to the community.

Work Experience

Department of Biological Sciences, Harvard College — **Cambridge, MA**
Senior Course Assistant, Biology 201 (plant physiology) and Biology 202 (animal behavior)
January 1997 to present; January 1996 to June 1996

- Supervise a weekly 5-hour core experimental laboratory course sequence required of all biology majors at Harvard College.
- Prepare and deliver a weekly 45-minute lecture and slide show on course material.
- Assist students with the design and execution of laboratory experiments.
- Teach statistical analysis of observed data sets to help students interpret outcomes.
- Provide mentoring and academic advising services to select group of students.

Department of Dermatology, Harvard Medical Center — **Cambridge, MA**
Undergraduate Researcher, focused on production of polyclonal antibodies
April 1996 to September 1996

- Developed and structured an independent project to identify the characterization of polyclonal antibodies.
- Used molecular biology techniques to collect and analyze data.
- Identified problems with past experimental protocols and developed new methods that resulted in more accurate and reliable experimentation.

Massachusetts General Hospital Diabetes Center — **Boston, MA**
Researcher, focusing on complications of diabetes mellitus, concentrating on the eye
June 1995 to September 1995

- Formed hypotheses, developed research methodology, and conducted tests to identify the effects of glucose concentration on pericyte growth.
- Measured results of tests to prove hypotheses and draw relevant conclusions.
- Acted as a team member at large, assisting other team members on experiments as needed.

Activities

Computer Consultant Intern, Harvard College — Spring 1996
Assisted members of the Harvard community with computer problems in a Macintosh-based computer cluster.

The Harvard Crimson **Columnist, Harvard College** — January 1995 to February 1996
Co-created and co-wrote "The Daily Grind," a satirical column that depicted the lives of five college students as they searched for good grades, romance, and some sort of explanation as to why they were getting neither.

Harvard Hotline Peer Counselor, Harvard College — 1993–1994
Fielded phone calls from members of the Harvard community who were upset, depressed, or just needed someone to talk to.

Resume 9: College Grad with CEO Ego

From Cocky . . .

This list references the numbered items on the next page:

1. Very strong academics.
2. Move dates to left column, under "Experience" to show chronology.
3. Including emptying the trash every evening?
4. Good—very results-oriented.
5. Define success.
6. Is this a soap opera or a resume? Consistent use of melodramatic terms is distracting and unprofessional.
7. Typo!
8. Doesn't sound like much of a team player.
9. Good, quantified.
10. Innovative.
11. A long time ago . . . probably not that important anymore. Why is he clinging to the past with so many more recent accomplishments?

"This resume is a great example of someone who thinks extremely highly of himself," says one of our reviewers. "The way it's worded shouts 'Me, Me, Me!' I'm immediately concerned that this person, although very accomplished, is not a team player and would not collaborate well with clients."

Although this is a strong resume as far as accomplishments go, we agree with this consultant that Richard's ego comes across as too forceful. Confidence is a good thing, but boastfulness is a problem. We've underlined and boxed the language that is particularly suggestive of an enormous ego. We suggest that Richard tone it down and make a few layout changes.

To make it easier to track his tenure at Clorox, we suggest that he move the dates to the left side of the page and mention the company name only once, at the top. His rapid career progression is impressive and should be highlighted.

In addition, he should move his state student award to the education section, where readers look for academic achievement. We caution against touting the awards earned in high school (and we've left it out of our re-write), but if he can't resist, he should include them in the activities section or under the high school mention.

To change the tone, we suggest eliminating the words "my" and "personally." Since this is his resume, we know it's what he did, otherwise it wouldn't be included. Other ways to alter the tone include eliminating words that don't add meaning, such as "superior," "significant," and "successful." For example "Developed a superior media plan" should be illustrated through the results of cutting 25 percent from the budget. We don't need Richard's opinion that his plan is superior.

Richard's resume would be stronger and much less irksome to a consultant reviewer if he stuck to his results, which are significant, and spared us the hype. His efforts to convince management of their mistakes might be a good learning experience to discuss in an interview, but such a mention on the resume raises red flags.

Richard M. Corbin ***18 Elm Street; Branford, CT 02130; (222)555–4005***

1 **EDUCATION** **Princeton, Princeton, NJ**
– Earned B.A. in English in May 1991. GPA: 3.9/4.0
– Graduated *magna cum laude* and with distinction from the English Department.
– Elected to Phi Beta Kappa after junior year (awarded to top 5% of class).
– Test scores: GMAT—750; SAT—760M, 660/v; Math I—800; Math II—800

Fieldview High School, Branford, CT
– Graduated 1st in a class of 253 in June 1987. GPA: 4.00/4.00

EXPERIENCE **Assistant Brand Manager, CLOROX**, September 1993 – June 1994 2

3 • Led every aspect of a International food product launch ($65 million annual sales potential).
– Created marketing plans which improved US project's NPV +92%, Profit +22%, and Volume +20%.
4 – Developed new TV ads with +49% higher trial potential than the strongest previously developed ads.
– Developed introductory sales plans which shipped 198% of 12-week objective.
5 – Successfully executed test plans (including Clorox Food's biggest ever Year I sampling plan).
– Led development of plans for launching this product in Canada, Mexico, England, and Japan.
– Consulted on international marketing issues; significantly improved launch plans in every country.

• Developed on my own initiative an enormously improved basic strategy for the Hidden Valley brand.
– Determined that a flanker strategy couldn't work for Hidden Valley. Recommended an equity strategy instead.
– For 30 months management rejected my recommendation, and consequently lost $38 million.
– After finally implementing my strategy, HV is seeing its first potentially positive results since 1988.

• Reversed Hidden Valley's 3 year share decline among US Hispanics
– Dramatically improved Hispanic advertising by reapplying successful ads from Anglo business.
– Developed a superior media plan which exceeded all objectives while cutting-25% from the budget.
– Identified opportunities to import products from Mexico. Project has $10 million NPV.

• Saved +$7.7 million by developing and implementing profit maximization plans on a struggling brand.
6 – Analyzed results of a recent food product initiative; concluded further spending would be futile.
– Gained management's agreement to my recommendation and implemented the plan successfully.

Brand Assistant, CLOROX, September 1993 – September 1993 7
– My supermarket marketing plans delivered +90% more recommendations than objective and went national.
– My in-home trial program for senior citizens shipped +50% more units than objective and went national.
– My Hispanic promotion plans grew our retail business +20% more than objective and paid out.
– Promoted to Assistant Brand Manager in September 1993.

Sales Management Intern, CLOROX
– Surpassed all sales quotas and job expectations. Sold 179 new items worth $100,000 annually. 9
– Managed 18 accounts. Developed persuasive selling skills.
Received full-time offer. Summer 1991.

Sales Representative, EASTERN IMPLEMENTS CORPORATION
– Developed winning price proposals in bidding situations. Fully managed sales and service for 25 accounts.
– Created scheduling processes which improved efficiency and ensured we met all deadlines. Summer 1990.

 **Co-Founder, STUDENT ADS COMPANY**

- Sold ad space on text book covers; distributed 2,000 covers to students.
- Personally sold $3,500 in ads on cold calls. Made a profit of $2,000 on sales of $5,250. Summer 1989.

ACTIVITIES **Independent Travel**, July 1995 – March 1996

6
- 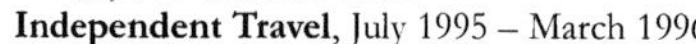 Fulfilled a lifelong dream by backpacking through Viet Nam, Thailand, India, Nepal, and Egypt.

Princeton Activities

- Co-edited a weekly humor and satire newsletter throughout 1991 and 1992.
- Elected by classmates to serve on Princeton's student body government. Led efforts to improve campus safety.
- Created a volunteer student escort service to operate nightly from 12:30 AM – 2:30 AM. 1990-91

 **AWARDS**

- State Student Fellowship; Awarded to 1 outstanding undergrad in Connecticut. 1991
- All-American Band & Jazz Band; Awarded to top 104 and 23 of 4,000+ applicants. 1988.
- Eagle Scout Rank; Earned from Boy Scouts of America. 1988.

. . . To Just the Facts

We've incorporated our suggested changes into our resume rewrite on the facing page. In the revised version, the recruiter will immediately see evidence of Robert's steady career progression without being distracted by the extraneous, self-congratulatory language he used to describe his achievements. Robert's achievements speak for themselves; as the second resume demonstrates, he doesn't need to beat the recruiter over the head with them.

However, the recruiter reviewing Robert's resume still might question the extent to which he is a team player; consulting recruiters like to see a record of measurable results, but they also know that consultants rarely achieve these results in isolation. It would be reassuring to see some evidence of teamwork on Robert's resume. By reframing a few of his accomplishments in a team-oriented context, Robert can polish his resume even further.

Richard M. Corbin

18 Elm Street, Branford, CT 02130
Tel: 222-555-4005; E-mail: rmcorbin@isp.com

EDUCATION

PRINCETON UNIVERSITY

- English B.A. in May 1991. GPA: 3.9.
- Graduated with high honors and with distinction from the English department.
- Elected to Phi Beta Kappa (awarded to top 5% of class) after junior year.
- GMAT score: 750.
- Elected by classmates to serve on Princeton's student body government.

EXPERIENCE

CLOROX CORPORATION

1993–1994

Assistant Brand Manager

- Led the international launch of a food product with projected annual sales of $65 million.
- Created marketing plans that improved U.S. project's net present value by 92%, profit by 22%, and sales volume by 20%.
- Developed new TV advertisements with 49% higher trial potential than previous ads.
- Developed introductory sales plans that resulted in achieving 198% of 12-week objective.
- Led development of plans for international product marketing and consulted on international marketing issues.
- Initiated and executed an equity strategy for Hidden Valley brand, which resulted in the brand's first positive sales growth since 1988.
- Saved $7.7 million by developing and implementing profit maximization plans on a struggling brand.

1992–1993

Brand Assistant

- Developed supermarket marketing plans that exceeded objectives by 90% and were adopted on a nationwide scale.
- Recommended and implemented an in-home trial program for senior citizens that exceeded sales objectives by 50% and was adopted on a nationwide scale.
- Devised improved promotion strategies to increase market share among Hispanics, resulting in retail sales growth exceeding projections by 20%.
- Promoted to assistant brand manager after one year.

Summer 1991

Sales Management Intern

- Managed 18 accounts and sold 179 new items worth $100,000 annually, exceeding personal sales quota.
- Received full-time employment offer at the completion of internship program.

Summer 1990

EASTERN IMPLEMENTS CORPORATION

Sales Representative

- Developed winning price proposals in bidding situations. Fully managed sales and service for 25 account.
- Created scheduling processes that improved efficiency and timeliness.

Summer 1989

STUDENT ADS COMPANY

Co-founder

- Sold ad space on textbook covers; distributed 2,000 covers to students.
- Personally sold $3,500 in ads through cold calls. Business made a total profit of $2,000.

ADDITIONAL

Recently spent eight months traveling throughout Asia; visited Vietnam, Thailand, India, Nepal and Egypt.

Cover Letters Reviewed

Now we will take a look at the cover letter. Although the cover letter is less important than the resume, you'll want to be sure that you don't send something in that will eliminate you from consideration. The first example below fills its role effectively. The second could easily cause trouble for the writer, regardless of her qualifications. By contrast, the third letter is brief but is also short on substance. We've included our suggestions and revisions with each of these cover letters.

Cover Letter Review 1

July 14, 2004

McKinsey & Company
Attention: Cathy Stevenson
75 Park Plaza
3rd Floor
Boston, Massachusetts 02116-3934

Dear Cathy:

Frank William suggested that I forward my resume to you for your consideration. I am a second-year MBA student at the Krannert Graduate School of Management at Purdue University, and I am currently working as a summer associate at Motorola in Chicago.

As Frank may have mentioned, I am in the top 5% of my class at Krannert, and I was recently elected President of the MBA student body. In and out of the classroom I have consistently demonstrated my capacity to make a positive impact regardless of the situation. My analytical and personal skills are ideally suited to management consulting, and I am confident that I would be an asset at McKinsey & Co.

I will call you next Wednesday to discuss next steps. If you do have any questions regarding my resume or qualifications, please do not hesitate to call. I look forward to speaking with you.

Sincerely:

Bill Pendleton

This is a very solid letter—clear, concise, and direct. We'd recommend just a few minor changes. If Bill wants to reach Cathy in person, he should contact her on Friday, since consultants are often in the office then (especially at many McKinsey offices). Otherwise he can leave a voice mail message, though that puts him at risk of initiating a game of phone tag, which can be frustrating for both parties. Bill should also check grammar carefully. Sticklers would note the improper use of the preposition "at" after the word asset. The proper wording is "I would be an asset to McKinsey & Co."

Cover Letter Review 2

From Way Too Much . . .

LINDA S. BRADFORD
305 Locust Drive #12, Los Angeles, CA 90046
310–555–0883

August 30, 2004

Hamilton Trout
Andersen Consulting
Spear Street Tower
One Market Plaza
Suite 3700
San Francisco, CA 94105

Dear Hamilton:

The purpose of this letter is to introduce myself to you and to present Andersen Consulting with the opportunity to increase profitability by securing my services as a professional. I have excellent academic and professional credentials, as reflected by my enclosed resume and Harvard Law School and undergraduate transcripts. Throughout my professional career, I have adhered to the highest standards of excellence and have demonstrated strong communication skills, analytical ability, poise, creativity, and dedication.

I am primed for a career change and the following explanation of my situation should give you some insight into my decision. After graduating from Harvard Law School, I gained extensive experience in high profile corporate litigation and counseling as a business litigator with two well-respected law firms, Rosenberg, Henredon & Spear and Letz, Milkum, Cheatum & Leave. In 1993, I returned to California to spend time with and care for my sister who was terminally ill. After my sister's death, I decided not to resume a "big firm" law practice so that I could explore business opportunities in the entertainment industry, while continuing to practice law as an independent contractor. Recently, after having spent sufficient time to have gained an insider's perspective, I concluded that I do not wish to continue pursuing a career in the entertainment industry. Rather, I desire to embark upon a business career at the level of sophistication that I was accustomed to in New York, primarily so that I can fully use my communication, analytical, and interpersonal skills, and because I genuinely miss the intellectual challenge, innovative thinking, pride in work product, and opportunity to provide the highest quality service to clients. Instead of resuming a purely legal career, I intend to translate my experience and abilities to the dynamic and productivity enhancing realm of business and management consulting. I have identified your firm, with its stellar reputation and corporate clientele, as an ideal match in light of my qualifications, work ethic, and interest. I am particularly interested in the Process and Strategic Services Competency Groups, and am very willing to travel extensively. I would prefer to be based on the West Coast, and am very interested in relocating to San Francisco.

I appreciate your time and attention and look forward to discussing with you and your colleagues a mutually beneficial association with Andersen Consulting. I am highly motivated and will provide quality results in a cost-effective manner. I would also appreciate your advice on the benefits of obtaining an M.B.A., which I am more than willing to pursue should this make me more useful to your firm. If I do not hear from you in the next several days, I will call to schedule a meeting.

Very truly yours,

Linda S. Bradford

encls.

"I couldn't get through the entire letter, given the daunting length and small font," one consultant tells us. "This is far too much information, and yet it doesn't tell me what I need to know: how her experience is relevant to consulting."

Aside from the verbosity, numerous red flags pop up to reviewers of this cover letter. The opening paragraph is almost silly in its confident tone. Most of our insiders agreed the first sentence was a real turn-off, which detracted from Linda's credentials. The long-winded explanation of her career path, including the mention of her sister's illness, reads like a novella and indicates that she has difficulty separating the important from the unimportant in the context of a cover letter. This is not a good quality in an aspiring consultant. Linda has gone to the trouble of including her transcripts, which are generally not necessary and serve to complicate and clutter her message. A GPA on her resume would suffice. She has even asked for advice on whether to pursue an MBA. By the time we've read the cover letter, we're pretty sure she's not cut out to be a consultant.

. . . To Short and Professional

We recommend the following rewrite, which is simple, clear, and to the point.

LINDA S. BRADFORD
305 Locust Drive #12
Los Angeles, CA 90046
310-555-0883

August 30, 2004

Hamilton Trout
Andersen Consulting
Spear Street Tower
One Market Plaza
Suite 3700
San Francisco, CA 94105

Dear Hamilton:

I am writing to introduce myself as a candidate for a consulting position at your firm. I have excellent academic and professional credentials, as indicated on my enclosed resume. Throughout my professional career, I have adhered to the highest standards of excellence and have demonstrated strong communication skills, analytical ability, poise, creativity, and dedication. [note - we need to then see clear evidence of these claims on the resume!]

Andersen's excellent reputation and corporate clientele are an ideal match with my interests. In particular, I believe my experience in formulating legal strategies and preparing analyses for complex litigation cases would be an excellent addition to your Strategic Services Competency Group.

I plan to be in San Francisco the week of September 15 and would like to meet with you then to further discuss my qualifications. I will call you on Friday and look forward to scheduling a meeting at your convenience in mid-September.

Very truly yours,

Linda S. Bradford

Cover Letter Review 3

From Generic . . .

Dear Ms. Conroy,

Through the www.careerbuilder.com website, I learned of your opportunity for a Senior Benefits Specialist. I am submitting my resume for your consideration.

I received my MBA in Management Information Systems and my BBA in Finance, Risk Management and Insurance from Temple University. For an MBA student–consulting project, I assisted in reviewing and redesigning the compensation structure for a suburban Philadelphia engineering firm.

For the past six years, I have worked at Aon Consulting, the 5th largest human resources consulting firm in the US. My primary responsibility is valuating retirement programs. I work on Qualified Pension Plans, Retiree Medical Plans, Supplemental Executive Retirement Programs, Deferred Compensation Plans, and Multi-employer Union Plans. Some projects that I have worked on include mergers and acquisitions, preparing benefit statements, calculating severance packages, projecting benefits, calculating FICA tax calculations for Executives, and conducting pay studies.

I look forward to discussing this opportunity with you and how my skills can be an asset to your company. I can be reached at (212) 555-6867 or via e-mail at graceadler@adler.com.

Sincerely,

Grace Adler

Rather than taking the time to incorporate her company- and job-specific research into a brief, compelling cover letter, this candidate has effectively written a Cliff Notes version of her resume. She's an actuarial analyst who wants to make a career transition into HR consulting, but she doesn't mention why she'd like to make the switch, or what interests her about this specific role or this particular company. In fact, there's no mention of the company to which she's applying anywhere on the letter. If we were the recruiter reviewing this cover message, we'd assume she was mass-mailing this cover letter in response to multiple postings, changing only the name of the recipient in the e-mail cover message. Brevity is indeed important in cover messages, but it's also important that your interest in the job comes across as well informed and sincere.

. . . To Targeted and Personalized

Here's our rewrite of Grace's cover letter, which explains specifically why she's interested in this position and this organization:

Dear Ms. Conroy,

Please allow me to introduce myself as Grace Adler, an applicant for the senior benefits consultant position in the Stamford office of Hewitt Associates. I learned of this opportunity through the CareerBuilder website, and based on the experience, skills, and qualifications outlined in the job announcement, I believe that I am well suited to join your team in this capacity.

As the attached resume indicates, I have spent the past two years working as an actuarial analyst with Aon Consulting; I was promoted into this role after my two-year tenure as a data analyst at the same firm. At Aon, I provide analysis and recommendations on a range of retirement investment vehicles, including qualified pension plans, retiree medical plans, supplemental executive retirement programs, and deferred compensation plans.

Now that I have developed a solid technical understanding of plan valuation and administration, I am eager to assume a more strategic advisory role in the creation, review, and redesign of competitive employee compensation packages. I am excited by the prospect of applying the client-facing, team-building, and results-oriented focus that have developed—as well as my familiarity with the employee benefits terrain—to a career with your organization. Not only does the senior benefits consultant position represent a logical next step in my desired career path, but it offers a unique opportunity to join a firm that is committed to providing both clients and employees with opportunities for continuous development and growth.

I would be delighted to meet you to discuss this opportunity further. Please feel free to contact me via return of e-mail or at the telephone number listed on the attached resume should you have any questions, or should you wish to schedule a time to speak about this position in greater detail.

Kindest regards,

Grace Adler

Cover Letter and Resume Pairs

Hopefully, the three examples we've provided have shown what distinguishes an effective cover letter from inbox clutter: Regardless of whether it's sent via e-mail, snail mail, or through your campus recruiting process, your cover message should be polite, concise, targeted, and personalized. Of course, the cover letter doesn't really stand on its own: It serves to set the stage for your resume and give the recipient a reason to scroll down and review your impressive qualifications. The following examples of resume and cover letter pairs show how the two work together to advance your case to the recruiter.

In our first example, the candidate is an experienced consultant looking to make a switch from one consulting firm pre-MBA to another firm post-MBA. This candidate doesn't necessarily need to belabor the point of why he's qualified to be a consultant; he's already *been* a consultant, and he knows he wants to continue along the consulting career track. The primary issue this candidate needs to address is why he's interested in this specific firm, and why he believes he'd thrive in the organization's unique culture.

By contrast, the second pair belongs to an undergraduate from a top school applying for an entry-level consultant position through an on-campus recruiting process. In this instance, the candidate is obviously capable: top school, great GPA, and evidence of leadership and extracurricular involvement. In his cover letter, he has to address the questions, "Why consulting?" and "Why this firm?" and create a link between his past accomplishments and his future consulting career.

Cover Letter/Resume Pair 1

Karen Walker
497 Jersey Avenue
Jersey City, NJ 07302
(551) 555-9771
k_walker@stern.xxx.edu

Mr. Jack McFarland
Recruiting Specialist
Kurt Salmon Associates, Inc.

September 23, 2004

Dear Mr. McFarland,

I am a second-year MBA student at New York University's Stern School of Business specializing in corporate finance and business strategy. I hope you will consider me for your closed invitation list when you interview candidates for your Growth & Profitability Solutions practice this fall.

As the attached resume indicates, I offer a consistent track record of successful team leadership over my six-year management consulting career. At both Arthur Andersen Business Consulting and BearingPoint, I led progressively larger teams of as many as eight consultants and twenty core client team members. Through my experiences on each of these teams, I have developed exceptional analytical skills, as well as the ability to leverage strategic thinking and effective team leadership to enable clients to successfully resolve their most pressing organizational challenges.

Though the consulting engagements on which I have worked have spanned numerous industries, I have developed a particular interest in the consumer products industry. To pursue this interest, I completed an internship with the Consumer Business practice of Deloitte Consulting this past summer. At Deloitte, I worked with a major health and beauty products company in Boston. This experience solidified my interest in consumer packaged goods, and I believe that my enthusiasm for (and experience with) this area of specialization will enable me to contribute significantly to the Kurt Salmon team.

In addition to highly relevant professional experience and proven analytical aptitude, I offer a sustained record of achievement in collaborative, team-based initiatives outside of the classroom as well. Through my conversations with current KSA team members, I have learned that consultants are actively encouraged to take on as much responsibility and initiative as they desire; I believe that my record of academic, professional, and extracurricular involvement will enable me to thrive in such an environment.

I look forward to meeting you and members of your team at your upcoming campus presentation, where I hope to learn more about this exciting opportunity. In the meantime, please feel free to contact me if you have any questions about my qualifications or should you wish to arrange a time to speak.

Sincerely,

Karen Walker

KAREN WALKER
497 Jersey Avenue
Jersey City, NJ 07302
Tel: 551-555-8071
E-mail: k_walker@stern.xxx.edu

Education:

NEW YORK UNIVERSITY New York, NY
Leonard N. Stern School of Business
Master of Business Administration, May 2005
Emphasis in Corporate Finance and Business Strategy

- Stern Scholar award recipient
- President, Stern Strategy & Operations Club
- VP, Stern Management Consulting Association & Director of Business Operations for a consulting trade magazine being developed by the club with planned circulation of 30,000+
- Member, Graduate Finance Association, Technology and New Media Group, Stern Soccer Club
- Finalist, Deloitte Consulting Casing Challenge
- Stern Consulting Corp – Completed program evaluation of Empowerment Business Incubation Initiative analyzing program's community impact and options for future organization

UNIVERSITY OF WISCONSIN Madison, WI
Bachelor of Science, Industrial Engineering, May 1997

- Dean's Honor List
- Member, Institute of Industrial Engineers and Society of Manufacturing Engineers

Experience:
Summer 2004

DELOITTE CONSULTING New York, NY
Summer Associate, Strategy & Operations

- Designed specifications and managed development of business reports and executive dashboards to meet client reporting needs as part of a Siebel 7.7 CRM implementation at a global CPG company.
- Facilitated the development of a new, integrated process for the approval and implementation of annual prices lists and customer-specific pricing changes.

2002-2003

BEARINGPOINT, INC. Milwaukee, WI
Senior Consultant, National Supply Chain Team

- Analyzed manufacturing process reliability related to a major new consumer product launch and identified a 30% gap between projected and target reliability. Designed system tests, implemented tracking system, and developed prioritized improvement plan to close gap before product launch.
- Developed and prioritized seven critical strategic initiatives and 56 other opportunities for a start-up medical equipment manufacturer resulting in streamlined operations and a technology map that forestalled a multi-million dollar systems investment for several years.
- Managed a team including four BearingPoint consultants, two subcontracted consultants and twelve core client team members to implement a shop floor control system at a high-tech manufacturer which provided component level product visibility, genealogy and traceability.

1997-2002

ARTHUR ANDERSEN BUSINESS CONSULTING Milwaukee, WI
Senior Consultant, Supply Chain Team

- Developed a financial reporting strategy articulation for a leading telecom equipment manufacturer including current state assessment, best practices benchmarking, and recommendations for more effective metrics, technology infrastructure and implementation timeline.
- Led a team to improve supply chain effectiveness at a $150 million industrial products manufacturer and recommended four initiatives with a net annual benefit over $5 million in revenue improvement and cost reduction.
- Managed four process improvement teams at a medical equipment manufacturer in the areas of product data management, service subcontracting, cycle counting, and inventory management. Improved inventory accuracy from 83% to 97% and improved service order processing time by 80% and error rate by 50%.
- Managed Baan IV ERP implementation teams at two industrial and automotive suppliers. Directed system configuration, data conversion, issue resolution, employee training and post go-live support.

Additional:

- Member, American Production and Inventory Control Society and Project Management Institute
- Certified in Production & Inventory Management (CPIM), Integrated Resource Management (CIRM)
- Other interests include soccer, basketball, reading and travel

Cover Letter/Resume Pair 2

Dear Mr. Spencer,

I am a senior at Yale University interested in applying for the undergraduate consultant position within Monitor's Marketspace practice. I learned of this opportunity through your posting on YaleLink, the online job database for undergraduates at Yale University. Based on the YaleLink announcement, I believe that I am particularly well suited for the consultant role.

At Yale, my concentration in Economics has required that I learn to use quantitative analysis and logical, strategic thinking as the basis for making informed business decisions and policy recommendations. Beyond the classroom, my extracurricular activities and professional experiences have enabled me to develop critical skills in three other important areas:

- **Problem-solving**—During my internship at a micro-credit bank last summer, I designed a new pension scheme for a women's cooperative bank. My success in this initiative required creative thinking, effective research, and a results-oriented focus on our client's needs.
- **Communication and teamwork**—As part of my micro-credit internship, I relied on strong communication skills to pitch funding proposals to major financial institutions such as Citibank and Bank of India. I also developed exceptional teamwork skills, as my position required extensive collaboration with other interns and bank staff.
- **Motivation and initiative**—At Yale, I have served on the board of the College Council for CARE (CCC)—an international development organization—for two consecutive years, and I have led the expansion of this group onto eight other college campuses.

I believe that my capabilities in these three areas will enable me to contribute significantly to a management consulting role after graduation. In particular, I am keenly interested in Monitor because of its unique focus on continuous learning and development. At the on-campus information session I attended last week, I was excited to hear current Monitor consultants describe the organization's formal mentoring program for new hires; because the consultant position itself involves such a steep learning curve, I am attracted to Monitor's firm-wide focus on one-on-one collaboration, relationship-building, and ongoing, on-the job training.

I am very interested in speaking with you to learn more about this exciting opportunity. Should you have any questions or should you wish to arrange a time to speak in greater detail, please feel free to contact me at (203) 555-6731. Otherwise, I will contact you via telephone in the next two weeks to see if it might be possible to schedule a meeting.

Kind regards,

Will Truman

WILL TRUMAN

School: P.O. Box 431, New Haven, CT 06520
Home: 420 Riverside Drive, New York, NY 10128
Phone: (203) 555-6731 • E-mail: truman@yale.edu

EDUCATION

Yale University, New Haven, CT
B.A. in Economics expected May 2005. GPA: 3.77 (GPA in Major: 3.85). SAT Math: 800 Verbal: 780.

American Chamber of Commerce Award for outstanding student combining excellence in scholarship with achievement in other fields.

EXPERIENCE

International Institute for Corporate Governance (Yale School of Management)
Research Assistant
July 2004-August 2004.
Assisted Director of the Institute and Finance Professor at Yale School of Management with research on how laws in over 90 countries limit expropriation of minority shareholders and creditors. Analyzed data and examined differences between common and civil law states. Coded corporate law of a range of countries and looked at how law was applied in specific cases of theft.

Mann Deshi Mahila Sanstha Bank (India)
Intern
June 2003-August 2003
Developed and launched pensions plan for an NGO/women's cooperative bank specializing in microcredit. Collected and analyzed data on the default rates of various branches of the bank, and used this research to revise loan criteria. Created publicity materials for program, and wrote proposals to procure more than $10,000 from Bank of India and Citibank.

Anglo-Eastern Shipping Management Co. (Hong Kong)
Temporary Allotment Officer
June 2002-August 2002
Coordinated correspondence with various banks (as well as India and UK offices) regarding allotments and remittances to be made to merchant navy officers. Audited accounts, updated databases, generated identification security cards using a computer program and completed administrative work.

EXTRACURRICULAR ACTIVITIES

College Council for CARE
Chair of Expansion; Publicity Manager & Campus Outreach Coordinator
September 2002-present
Initiated national expansion of this youth initiative began at Yale for CARE international – a humanitarian agency working to alleviate poverty in developing countries. Organized a conference to educate our campus and teach 8 other schools how to set up chapters. Publicized events held on-campus to fundraise for CARE international or educate the local community.

Social Entrepreneurs
Online Resource Centre Chair
September 2002-December 2003
Researched resources and information on social entrepreneurship, posted online materials. Attended lectures at Yale School of Management and helped graduate students develop their business plans for consulting local non-profits.

Student Campaign for Child Survival
On-Campus Fundraising Officer
January 2002-January 2003
Wrote applications requesting foreign aid to fund vaccines for children in developing countries. Also worked on outreach and nationwide expansion.

PERSONAL

Fluent in English and Hindi, proficient in Chinese (Mandarin) and intermediate (GCSE) level French. Play violin; write theatre reviews for *Yale Daily News*; practice Tae Kwon Do; act as mentor for international students; volunteer with on-campus peer counseling hotline.

Getting Your Foot in the Door

Now that you have a great resume, what should you do with it? Consulting firms receive resumes through three primary channels: campus recruiting programs, employee recommendations, and "over the transom"—directly from a candidate, unsolicited or in response to an ad. Insiders tell us that your chances of getting an interview vary significantly depending on which channel you use. But whatever the channel, timing is very important. It's best to investigate the firm's recruiting cycle, which usually gears up around October for full-time hires or January for summer hires. This is when firms are most likely hiring and determining the headcount they'll need the following year.

Campus Recruiting

The best way to get into a firm is to go through the campus interviewing process. All top firms purchase resume books from graduate schools and select candidates to interview from those. They also interview on many campuses. Most firms actively recruit at top colleges and business schools. Some, McKinsey for example, also look at top JD and PhD programs. These days, firms are very anxious to get the best and brightest people, and since they are already expending the energy to come to a campus to interview candidates, they feel they should interview as many as possible. If you aren't selected by the firm for an interview, bid what points you must to obtain an interview. But if for some reason you are not able to get an interview while your chosen firm is at your campus, you should try calling the local office recruiting contact. He or she can probably fit you in before or after that day's scheduled appointments or arrange to squeeze you in some other time. If recruiters like what they see on your resume, they will often try to help you in this way. Remember, they are as eager to hire top people as you are to work for their firm.

If the firm you're targeting does recruit on your campus, it's a good idea to attend the information sessions usually offered a few weeks before interviews. Many insiders we spoke with said they were more likely to spend extra time reading a resume and even giving the benefit of the doubt to a candidate who had expressed interest in the firm by attending events and making an effort to meet some of the consultants there.

Personal Contact

If you're not currently in school, or if you are, but not at one where firms recruit, you're going to have a greater challenge on your hands. Insiders unanimously agree that your best bet is to try to find someone you know at the firm or someone who has a contact at the firm. Look into your school alumni directories to see if any graduates are working there. Or get a contact name in the practice area in which you have relevant experience. Call the switchboard and ask for names if you must!

The best route is to call the contact person, give him or her your 15-second resume summary, and ask for information about the firm. You have two objectives in doing this: to get more information on the firm to use in your interview, and to get that person to ask for your resume so he or she can forward it to the right person.

Why would someone who doesn't know you do this for you? Money. Many firms give employee referral bonuses. "If I refer somebody who gets hired as a consultant, I get a $5,000 bonus," explains one insider. "So I have a big incentive to help bring in the right people."

Once you have a contact, send your resume to that person. Ideally, the contact will forward the resume to the person who reviews resumes and schedules interviews, with a note asking that an interview be granted. There's always the risk that the contact will think you're not the right fit, in which case you won't be recommended. Don't worry. Your contact is not the only person who reviews resumes. Most firms recruit in a decentralized system. You have many more doors to knock on, in different practice areas, depending on the size of the office, and in different offices within the firm.

Insiders tell us that an employee recommendation strongly affects the decision whether to interview a candidate. Though we don't have statistics, all agree that your chances of getting an interview through a personal contact go way up, even if your resume is less than stellar. With a stellar resume and a recommendation, you're probably a shoo-in.

Over the Transom

If you strike out in the personal contact arena, your resume really counts. It's the only tool you have to sell yourself, and it represents your only chance to get a foot in the door (though the multiple-door theory still holds—if one closes, another can be opened). When submitting your resume, whether in response to a job listing or without solicitation, target firms that are likely to be interested in your background. Your resume will most likely be screened by an administrator for the "required four," then forwarded to a recruiter in the specific practice area. Specialization, to the greatest extent possible, is probably your best angle. You have a better chance of getting an interview if someone with a similar background, who has needs in your area of expertise, reads your resume.

Following Up

One head of recruiting confesses, "The biggest pains-in-the-asses finally do get interviews." We don't advocate becoming a nuisance, but there is something to be said for persistence. After all, as we said above, many firms look for people who take initiative and are good problem solvers. You get the picture.

Here are a few basic rules for following up once you've sent your resume:

- Be persistent but not pesky—two calls in 1 day are overkill; two calls in 1 week are probably fine.
- Be prescriptive in your requests—ask specifically for what you want, whether it's to schedule an interview or have a casual chat on the phone.
- Keep the ball in your court—you'll probably feel more in control if you can plan the next steps rather than wait by the phone.
- Make yourself easily available—provide a number where a message can be left at any time; if possible, plan to travel to the firm's office for a meeting at your expense.

The Phone Fandango

Insiders tell us that one of the most difficult things to do is return phone calls while on the road. Put yourself in the shoes of the average consultant with recruiting responsibility. You're at the client site at least 4 days a week, with the possibility of Fridays in your office. You're under a Friday deadline. The analysts are behind schedule due to a software glitch. The client is getting antsy about the amount of change that might be required. The head of your practice has scheduled an impromptu visit to check in on the project tomorrow. Your significant other is mad because you forgot to call last night. . . .

Here's what happens when a consultant listens to your voice mail at 11:53 p.m. Wednesday:

You: This is Susan Brown calling on Wednesday at 10 a.m. I sent you my resume on Monday and wondered whether you'd had a chance to take a look at it. I'll be in all day today, at (333) 555-8956.

Consultant thinks: Who is Susan Brown and why is she calling me?

The consultant has certainly not seen the resume—he hasn't even been in the office since last Friday. And he surely doesn't have time to return your call without committing a time-zone foul. When he finally gets a few minutes free with access to a phone, he's more likely to call his significant other or pet poodle than to return a phantom resume call.

Message Magic

If you plan to call, here are some better approaches:

You: This is Susan Brown calling on Wednesday. At Sandy Smith's request, I sent my resume to you on Monday. I would like to schedule an interview and will call you on Friday to discuss my qualifications.

Consultant thinks: I'll deal with this Friday if I have time in the office.

This is an improvement. Now at least the consultant can be on the lookout for the resume and has some incentive to do so, because Sandy is a friend and colleague.

You: This is Susan Brown calling. I recently sent my resume to you and would like to discuss my qualifications. I have 4 years' experience working in the packaged foods industry as a manufacturing engineer and I recently received my MBA from the Fuqua School at Duke University. I will call back next week once you've had a chance to review my resume so we can schedule a time to meet.

Consultant thinks: I'd better look for this resume. We're always looking for manufacturing experience.

This is good. Presuming you have done your homework and contacted a consultant in either the packaged foods or manufacturing practice area of the firm, the consultant is at least likely to try to find your resume and read it.

A good idea for your second follow-up call next week might go something like this:

You: This is Susan Brown, the candidate with manufacturing experience in packaged foods and an MBA from Fuqua. I'll be in Boston this Friday and would like to meet with you to discuss my qualifications if your schedule allows. If you would call me back and let me know if it would be possible to arrange a short meeting on Friday, I would appreciate it. You may leave a message for me any time at (333) 555-8956, or I will call you Friday morning to make plans then.

Consultant thinks: Hmm, I remember this resume and it's probably worth seeing her. I'll check my schedule and leave a message for her this evening.

You left another brief summary of your experience so the consultant would remember seeing the resume. You were specific about your plans to be in Boston on Friday, which gives the consultant an opportunity to interview you without having to pay your airfare.

If you've left a message and your call hasn't been returned, don't hesitate to call again. Remember, consultants are usually fully booked during the day and often work late into the night, when the last thing on their minds is returning resume calls. The best tactic is to be persistent and pleasant without badgering. Most insiders we spoke with said they usually make an effort at least to return a call, even if they aren't interested in interviewing the candidate. Don't give up until you've tried at least three times over 2 weeks to contact the consultant.

If you've left three messages and all have been ignored, you may want to send your resume to someone else and start the process again. Another option is to contact an administrator in the office, or the consultant's assistant if one exists, and determine the best method of contacting your target. Many firms communicate primarily through voice mail, although you might have luck using e-mail or even leaving a good old-fashioned message with the secretary. Tailor your approach to what you have learned about how the particular firm communicates.

Note: If you don't reach the consultant, your treatment of the recruiting administrator should be positive and respectful. Treat any person at the firm the same way you would the professional responsible for reviewing your resume. We know of more than one candidate rejected by the recruiting administrator because of an attitude!

Interview Prep

Many insiders tell us they develop case study questions according to experience mentioned on a candidate's resume. This is especially true for undergraduates, who are generally not expected to have broad industry knowledge but are expected to be able to analyze an industry they've worked in, for example.

The best way to prepare for the first interview is to know your resume extremely well. Prepare your 20- to 30-second spiel to familiarize your interviewer with your background and major accomplishments. You should be able to describe points on your resume in a clear, concise, and convincing manner. You should also be prepared to discuss each area of your "Experience" section, providing details and insight wherever possible. Consultants want evidence that you are thoughtful about your experience—both successes and failures—and that you demonstrate a capacity to learn and grow as you progress.

Resume Blunders

As we have mentioned, your resume will help the interviewer identify areas to probe during the first interview. In particular, consultants will look for weaknesses or inconsistencies to check, and may even formulate questions or cases directed at your resume weaknesses. Read your resume with a critical eye, looking for things that might appear odd or inconsistent. Use the list below to help you identify those areas that are of particular concern to consultants.

Time Gaps

One reason consultants like chronological resumes is that they want to know whether a candidate took time off between school years or jobs. Time off is not necessarily a bad thing, but you need to be prepared to explain any lapses between jobs or between your sophomore and junior year, for example. If you traveled, be prepared to describe something you learned during that time. If you took time off to have a baby, resolve a personal issue, or "find yourself," you need to practice your answer to the time gap question. It's usually best not to go into a lot of personal detail—insiders tell us this is a warning sign, especially in the first interview. But be clear and focus on what you accomplished during that time. Firms want to be sure you can handle the normal rigors of 4 or more years in academia, jobs with increasing responsibility, and balancing your personal and professional lives.

Inconsistent Performance

If your accomplishments appear strong in one area and weak in another—1200 on the SATs with a 3.2 GPA, honors graduate of a top school with no notable professional accomplishments—you should expect questions about this disparity. The interviewer will want to know the reason behind your low GPA (did you work part time during school?) or your mediocre experience. Be prepared to explain any circumstances that impacted your performance, but again, avoid undue personal detail.

Career Hopping

If you've been at several companies in just a few years, or never stayed at one company longer than a year or two, you risk being perceived as a job-hopper. Your interviewer may wonder whether you've been fired for poor performance. Frequent career changes sometimes indicate that a person has difficulty sticking with a situation, working through problems, or committing to a job. All of these are obvious concerns to consultants, whose work requires tenacity and a strong commitment to delivering client value. In addition, most consulting firms look for people who want to stay around for a while. Three years is often considered a break-even point, but many firms would like individuals with longer-term tenure in mind.

Former Consultants

If you've been a consultant before and are interviewing with another firm, expect questions about your interest in the new firm and your continued commitment to a career in consulting. "The early years as a consultant involve paying your dues," says one insider. "I always question a candidate who has left a firm after a few years and now is interviewing here. I assume they were forced out and I'm skeptical of their consulting ability." Most insiders said they were eager to talk to experienced consultants, but that they definitely quiz the candidate's motive for leaving a former firm.

Local Yokels

If you've spent most of your academic and professional life in Boston, you may be questioned about your sudden interest in joining the Chicago office of a firm. This is especially true for those who have attended school and worked in California. Midwest and East Coast firms have a terrible time getting these candidates to relocate, and in some cases they have all but given up trying. A firm that must fly you out for an interview will probably quiz you over the phone before anteing up. And relocation costs, often paid by the firm, are reserved for candidates who demonstrate a real commitment to the new locale and are prepared to make the inevitable lifestyle compromises that come with relocating.

Next Steps

At this point, you've learned what resume reviewers are looking for as they scan the all-important 1-page summary of your life. You've reviewed the standard consulting resume structure and format, and you've considered how to tie your academic, extracurricular, and professional experiences together in a way that would persuade even the most cynical consulting recruiter to give you one of a few prized interview slots. You've reviewed the sample resumes and cover letters in this guide, and you're confident that you can now discern the ordinary resumes from the extraordinary ones. Now what?

We've compiled the following list of suggested next steps, as well as a few other resources and publications that jobseekers have found helpful as they've navigated the recruiting process.

Suggested Next Steps

Students: Visit Your Career Center

Most career-placement offices at both colleges and business schools offer resume consultations, resume- and cover letter–writing workshops, and one-on-one mock interview practice sessions. Many of them also compile binders of resumes from current and former students that are readily available for your reference. Take advantage of these! Even if all of the resources at the career planning offices are general rather than consulting-specific, you'll take home a lot of valuable information about effective resume writing and interviewing. Successful candidates—particularly those who've endured the notoriously rigorous recruiting process for management consulting—take all of the help that they can get as they prepare for interviews.

Research the Consulting Industry

Even if you've read all of WetFeet's resources on consulting, be sure to keep your industry knowledge up to date. A general resource for information about the consulting industry is *Consultants News*, published by Kennedy Information. For more information about this and other Kennedy publications, visit ConsultingCentral.com or the Kennedy Information website, www.kennedyinfo.com. Though a subscription to the publication (required for online access to content) costs a hefty $349 a year, current and back issues of *Consultants News* may be available through your business school library; if they are, this publication is definitely worth a look for the otherwise hard-to-find information on industry and firm-specific trends and developments.

Reading *Fast Company*, *Fortune*, *Forbes*, *Business Week*, *Business 2.0*, the *Wall Street Journal*, and the *New York Times* is also an easy way to stay up-to-date on the latest events and issues that management consultants address, and will arm you with plenty of information for your interviews. Each of these publications has a corresponding website that's worth a visit. If you're currently a student and your library offers access to Factiva (an online database that offers full-text articles from thousands of individual publications, including all of those listed in the Reference section of this book), you can search for industry-specific and company-specific news to prepare for interviews. Plunkett Research—another online database—also offers a wealth of information about the consulting industry, including detailed profiles of consulting firms, white papers that describe the trends shaping the industry, and industry-specific interview tips. If your campus library offers Plunkett Research Online—or if it offers the print versions of its consulting industry guide—it's worth taking a look at these resources in advance of your interviews. If you're pressed for time and need a quick-and-dirty synopsis of a particular firm, take a look at the Hoover's online database (www.hoovers.com).

Read Firm-Specific Literature

As you write your cover letter and resume, be sure to check out any firm-specific literature you can find. This includes the WetFeet Insider Guides to consulting firms (see the list at the end of this book), which provide insights into the firms' areas of relative strength and insiders' perceptions of the companies' culture. In addition, be sure to review any recruiting literature on file at your campus career center. This information is likely to be fairly general, but it will provide a useful overview of each firm's organizational structure and respective recruiting processes. Also, these materials will give you a general sense of the employment brand that the firm is trying to convey—in other words, you'll get a sense of how the firm distinguishes itself from other firms in the marketplace that compete for talent.

Visit Company Websites

Check out the website of each firm to which you're applying. This does not mean that you'll be expected to memorize and regurgitate either the company's financials or its business principles in the course of the interview. However, if you're interviewing with a public company, you should probably at least take a gander at the firm's annual report (generally available through the "Investor Relations" section of the firm's website). In addition to providing detailed information on the company's financials, the annual report highlights the key transactions in which the bank was involved over the course of the previous year and summarizes the relative performance of each of its major revenue-generating areas. Also, check out the most recent press releases for any noteworthy developments that have taken place since the last annual report went to press.

Attend On-Campus Information Sessions

Trust us: The hour that you spend at each firm's on-campus meet-and-greet will be time well spent. At the information session, the company will undoubtedly address the topic of what sets it apart from its chief competitors—its competitors for business and its competitors for talented people. In addition, these information sessions provide an opportunity for you to meet current consultants and to hear them answer the questions that you've been formulating throughout the course of your research.

Take the Time to Speak with Insiders!

There's really no substitute for good old-fashioned informational networking (a process which should be relatively easy for current MBA students, who have a considerable network of B-school students, former consultants, summer interns, and alumni to consult). If you're an undergrad with fewer industry contacts, check out your career center's alumni database for the names and contact details of current firm employees (preferably within the practice area to which you're applying).

Additional Resources

WetFeet Resources

Visit WetFeet.com to get help on everything from finding the right firm to acing your case. There you will find:

- Articles on writing killer cover letters and resumes
- Tips on putting your best foot forward in your interviews
- Guides to specific consulting firms
- An in-depth Insider Guide series on how to ace your case interviews
- Plus a wide range of topical information relevant to your job

In particular, you might find WetFeet's Insider Guide to *Careers in Management Consulting* helpful. In this popular Insider Guide, you'll explore:

- Profiles of 37 top strategy, Big Four, and specialty consulting firms.
- Consulting opportunities beyond McKinsey and BCG.
- Which firm is right for you—based on our exclusive Consulting Firm Appeal Test.
- The latest industry trends.
- Industry rankings of the major firms.
- A week in the life of a typical consultant.
- The typical career paths at the different firms.
- How to prepare for the recruiting process, including the dreaded case interview.
- Key differences between working for a consulting firm vs. an investment bank.

Books

The Fast Track: The Insider's Guide to Winning Jobs in Management Consulting, Investment Banking, and Securities Trading

Mariam Naficy (Broadway, 1997)

Though outdated, this book still provides an excellent overview of careers in management consulting. As the name implies, this book is a particularly good resource for those for those candidates comparing potential opportunities in multiple areas.

Consultants News *Career Guide to the Top Consulting Firms*

(Kennedy Information, 2000)

This reference guide—published by Kennedy Information, the primary source of competitive intelligence and market analysis on the consulting industry—is also somewhat outdated, but is definitely worth a look if you're preparing yourself for the consulting firm recruiting process. Based on dozens of interviews with current and former consultants at 25 top firms, the book includes information on the corporate culture at various firms, typical career paths, relative compensation, firm histories, and recruiting process.

The Overnight Resume

Donald Asher (Ten Speed Press, 1999)

The author of this book, Donald Asher, is also the author of *Asher's Bible of Executive Resumes and How to Write Them*, long considered a must-read reference book for senior-level professionals looking to switch jobs. In *The Overnight Resume*, Asher offers guidance on writing a clear, concise, and targeted resume that reflects the individual candidate's specific career objectives. It doesn't include much in the way of industry-specific resume guidance, but it's worthwhile supplemental reading if you need additional ideas to get you started.

And even if you feel confident that your resume is in ship-shape, check out the book's cartoons—they're guaranteed to inject a little bit of brevity and humor into an otherwise tedious and stressful job-search experience.

Get the Interview Every Time

Brenda Greene (Dearborn Trade Publishing, 2004)

This book offers advice based on interviews with more than 50 Fortune 500 employers, who share their insights on what commands their attention (and what gets on their nerves) when they review resumes. This guide isn't consulting-industry specific (in fact, few consulting firms made the list of companies that Greene surveyed), but it is packed with useful job search information nonetheless. It includes several sample resumes and cover letters that represent what hiring managers, directors, and vice presidents want to see, and it includes practical guidance on how to research companies and opportunities before sending any resumes; how to distill your experiences into the constraints of a 1-page resume and cover letter; and how to design and submit an electronic resume correctly.

WETFEET'S INSIDER GUIDE SERIES

JOB SEARCH GUIDES

Getting Your Ideal Internship

Job Hunting A to Z: Landing the Job You Want

Killer Consulting Resumes!

Killer Investment Banking Resumes!

Killer Cover Letters & Resumes!

Negotiating Your Salary & Perks

Networking Works!

INTERVIEW GUIDES

Ace Your Case: Consulting Interviews

Ace Your Case II: 15 More Consulting Cases

Ace Your Case III: Practice Makes Perfect

Ace Your Case IV: The Latest & Greatest

Ace Your Case V: Return to the Case Interview

Ace Your Interview!

Beat the Street: Investment Banking Interviews

Beat the Street II: I-Banking Interview Practice Guide

CAREER & INDUSTRY GUIDES

Careers in Accounting

Careers in Advertising & Public Relations

Careers in Asset Management & Retail Brokerage

Careers in Biotech & Pharmaceuticals

Careers in Brand Management

Careers in Consumer Products

Careers in Entertainment & Sports

Careers in Human Resources

Careers in Information Technology

Careers in Investment Banking

Careers in Management Consulting

Careers in Manufacturing

Careers in Marketing & Market Research

Careers in Nonprofits & Government Agencies

Careers in Real Estate

Specialized Consulting Careers: Health Care, Human Resources & Information Technology

Careers in Supply Chain Management

Careers in Venture Capital

Consulting for PhDs, Doctors & Lawyers

Industries & Careers for MBAs

Industries & Careers for Undergrads

COMPANY GUIDES

Accenture

Bain & Company

Boston Consulting Group

Booz Allen Hamilton

Citigroup's Corporate & Investment Bank

Credit Suisse First Boston

Deloitte Consulting

Goldman Sachs Group

J.P. Morgan Chase & Company

Lehman Brothers

McKinsey & Company

Merrill Lynch

Morgan Stanley

25 Top Consulting Firms

Top 20 Biotechnology & Pharmaceuticals Firms

Top 25 Financial Services Firms